psalms

the book of

psalms

authorised king james version

printed by authority

published by canongate

with an introduction by | bono

First published in Great Britain in 1999
by Canongate Books Ltd
14 High Street, Edinburgh EH1 1TE

10 9 8 7 6 5 4 3 2 1

Introduction copyright © Bono 1999
The moral right of the author has been asserted

British Library Cataloguing-in-Publication Data
A catalogue record is available on request from
the British Library

ISBN 0 86241 969 7

Typeset by Palimpsest Book Production
Book design by Paddy Cramsie at et al
Printed and bound in Great Britain
by Caledonian International, Bishopbriggs

a note about pocket canons

The Authorised King James Version of the Bible, translated between 1603–11, coincided with an extraordinary flowering of English literature. This version, more than any other, and possibly more than any other work in history, has had an influence in shaping the language we speak and write today.

Twenty-four of the eighty original books of the King James Bible are brought to you in this series. They encompass categories as diverse as history, philosophy, law, poetry and fiction. Each Pocket Canon also has its own introduction, specially commissioned from an impressive range of writers, to provide a personal interpretation of the text and explore its contemporary relevance.

introduction by bono

Bono was born (Paul David Hewson) in Dublin in 1960. At seventeen he joined the embryonic U2 with three school-friends. U2 released their first record with Island Records in April 1980 and have gone on to sell 87 million albums worldwide, gathering seven Grammies in the US and five Brit Awards in the UK along the way. In 1992 their ground-breaking Zoo TV tour was hailed as the most innovative spectacle ever staged. The follow-up, 1997's Pop-Mart tour, built on that inventiveness, and played to a record-breaking four million people worldwide. In 1994 Bono was invited to present the Lifetime Achievement Award to Frank Sinatra at the Grammies. He was the guest speaker at the UK International Year of Literature in 1995. The Million Dollar Hotel, a film based on a story co-written by Bono, is currently in production starring Mel Gibson and directed by Wim Wenders. Bono lives in Dublin with his wife and three children.

Explaining belief has always been difficult. How do you explain a love and logic at the heart of the universe when the world is so out of whack? How about the poetic versus the actual truth found in the scriptures? Has free will got *us* crucified? And what about the dodgy characters who inhabit the tome, known as the bible, who claim to hear the voice of God?

You have to be interested, but is God?

Explaining faith is impossible … Vision over visibility … Instinct over intellect … A songwriter plays a chord with the faith that he will hear the next one in his head.

One of the writers of the psalms was a musician, a harp-player whose talents were required at 'the palace' as the only medicine that would still the demons of the moody and insecure King Saul of Israel; a thought that still inspires, if not quite explaining Marilyn singing for Kennedy, or the Spice Girls in the court of Prince Charles …

At age 12, I was a fan of David, he felt familiar … like a pop star could feel familiar. The words of the psalms were as poetic as they were religious and he was a star. A dramatic character, because before David could fulfil the prophecy and become the king of Israel, he had to take quite a beating. He was forced into exile and ended up in a cave in some no-name border town facing the collapse of his ego and abandonment by God. But this is where the soap opera got interesting, this is where David was said to have composed his first psalm – a blues. That's what a lot of the psalms feel like to me, the blues. Man shouting at God – 'My God, my God why hast thou forsaken me? Why art thou so far from helping me?' (Psalm 22).

I hear echoes of this holy row when un-holy bluesman Robert Johnson howls 'There's a hellhound on my trail' or Van Morrison sings 'Sometimes I feel like a motherless child'. Texas Alexander mimics the psalms in 'Justice Blues':

'I cried Lord my father, Lord eh Kingdom come. Send me back my woman, then thy will be done'. Humorous, sometimes blasphemous, the blues was backslidin' music; but by its very opposition, flattered the subject of its perfect cousin Gospel.

Abandonment, displacement, is the stuff of my favourite psalms. The Psalter may be a font of gospel music, but for me it's in his despair that the psalmist really reveals the nature of his special relationship with God. Honesty, even to the point of anger. 'How long, Lord? Wilt thou hide thyself forever?' (Psalm 89) or 'Answer me when I call' (Psalm 5).

Psalms and hymns were my first taste of inspirational music. I liked the words but I wasn't sure about the tunes – with the exception of Psalm 23, 'The Lord is my Shepherd'. I remember them as droned and chanted rather than sung. Still, in an odd way, they prepared me for the honesty of John Lennon, the baroque language of Bob Dylan and Leonard Cohen, the open throat of Al Green and Stevie Wonder – when I hear these singers, I am reconnected to a part of me I have no explanation for … my 'soul' I guess.

Words and music did for me what solid, even rigorous, religious argument could never do, they introduced me to God, not belief in God, more an experiential sense of GOD. Over art, literature, reason, the way in to my spirit was a combination of words and music. As a result the Book of *Psalms* always felt open to me and led me to the poetry of *Ecclesiastes*, the *Song of Solomon*, the book of *John* … My religion could not be fiction but it had to transcend facts. It could be mystical, but not mythical and definitely not ritual …

bono

My mother was Protestant, my father Catholic; anywhere other than Ireland that would be unremarkable. The 'Prods' at that time had the better tunes and the Catholics had the better stage-gear. My mate Gavin Friday used to say: 'Roman Catholicism is the Glamrock of religion' with its candles and psychedelic colours ... Cardinal blues, scarlets and purples, smoke bombs of incense and the ring of the little bell. The Prods were better at the bigger bells, they could afford them. In Ireland wealth and Protestantism went together; to have either, was to have collaborated with the enemy, i.e. Britain. This did not fly in our house.

After going to Mass at the top of the hill, in Finglas on the north side of Dublin, my father waited outside the little Church of Ireland chapel at the bottom of the hill, where my mother had brought her two sons ...

I kept myself awake thinking of the clergyman's daughter and let my eyes dive into the cinema of the stained glass. These Christian artisans had invented the movies ... light projected through colour to tell their story. In the '70s the story was 'the Troubles' and the Troubles came through the stained glass; with rocks thrown more in mischief than in anger, but the message was the same; the country was to be divided along sectarian lines. I had a foot in both camps, so my Goliath became religion itself; I began to see religion as the perversion of faith. As to the five smooth stones for the sling ... I began to see God everywhere else. In girls, fun, music, justice but still – despite the lofty King James translation – the scriptures ...

I loved these stories for the basest reasons, not just the

New Testament with its mind-altering concept that God might reveal himself as a baby born in straw poverty – but even the Old Testament. These were action movies, with some hardcore men and women ... the car chases, the casualties, the blood and guts; there was very little kissing ...

David was a star, the Elvis of the bible, if we can believe the chiselling of Michelangelo (check the face – but I still can't figure out this most famous Jew's foreskin). And unusually for such a 'rock star', with his lust for power, lust for women, lust for life, he had the humility of one who knew his gift worked harder than he ever would. He even danced naked in front of his troops ... the biblical equivalent of the royal walkabout. David was definitely more performance artist than politician.

Anyway, I stopped going to churches and got myself into a different kind of religion. Don't laugh, that's what being in a rock 'n' roll band is, not pseudo-religion either ... Show-business is Shamanism: Music is Worship; whether it's worship of women or their designer, the world or its destroyer, whether it comes from that ancient place we call soul or simply the spinal cortex, whether the prayers are on fire with a dumb rage or dove-like desire ... the smoke goes upwards ... to God or something you replace God with ... usually yourself.

Years ago, lost for words and forty minutes of recording time left before the end of our studio time, we were still looking for a song to close our third album, *War*. We wanted to put something explicitly spiritual on the record to balance the politics and the romance of it; like Bob Marley or Marvin

Gaye would. We thought about the psalms ... 'Psalm 40' ... There was some squirming. We were a very 'white' rock group, and such plundering of the scriptures was taboo for a white rock group unless it was in the 'service of Satan'. Or worse, Goth.

'Psalm 40' is interesting in that it suggests a time in which grace will replace karma, and love replace the very strict laws of Moses (i.e. fulfil them). I love that thought. David, who committed some of the most selfish as well as selfless acts, was depending on it. That the scriptures are brim full of hustlers, murderers, cowards, adulterers and mercenaries used to shock me; now it is a source of great comfort.

'40' became the closing song at U2 shows and on hundreds of occasions, literally hundreds of thousands of people of every size and shape t-shirt have shouted back the refrain, pinched from 'Psalm 6': "'How long' (to sing this song)". I had thought of it as a nagging question – pulling at the hem of an invisible deity whose presence we glimpse only when we act in love. How long ... hunger? How long ... hatred? How long until creation grows up and the chaos of its precocious, hell-bent adolescence has been discarded? I thought it odd that the vocalising of such questions could bring such comfort; to me too.

But to get back to David, it is not clear how many, if any, of these psalms David or his son Solomon really wrote. Some scholars suggest the royals never dampened their nibs and that there was a host of Holy Ghost writers ... Who cares? I didn't buy Leiber and Stoller ... they were just his songwriters ... I bought Elvis.

the book of psalms

1
Blessed is the man that walketh not
    in the counsel of the ungodly,
nor standeth in the way of sinners,
    nor sitteth in the seat of the scornful.
² But his delight is in the law of the Lord;
    and in his law doth he meditate day and night.
³ And he shall be like a tree planted
    by the rivers of water,
        that bringeth forth his fruit in his season;
his leaf also shall not wither;
    and whatsoever he doeth shall prosper.
⁴ The ungodly are not so, but are like the chaff
    which the wind driveth away.
⁵ Therefore the ungodly shall not stand
    in the judgment,
        nor sinners in the congregation
of the righteous.
⁶ For the Lord knoweth the way of the righteous;
    but the way of the ungodly shall perish.

2
Why do the heathen rage,
    and the people imagine a vain thing?

2 The kings of the earth set themselves, and the rulers
   take counsel together, against the Lord,
      and against his anointed, saying,
3 'Let us break their bands asunder,
   and cast away their cords from us.'
4 He that sitteth in the heavens shall laugh:
   the Lord shall have them in derision.
5 Then shall he speak unto them in his wrath,
   and vex them in his sore displeasure.
6 Yet have I set my king
   upon my holy hill of Zion.
7 I will declare the decree:
   the Lord hath said unto me,
      'Thou art my Son;
   this day have I begotten thee.
8 Ask of me, and I shall give thee the heathen
   for thine inheritance,
      and the uttermost parts of the earth
   for thy possession.
9 Thou shalt break them with a rod of iron;
   thou shalt dash them in pieces
      like a potter's vessel.'
10 Be wise now therefore, O ye kings:
   be instructed, ye judges of the earth.
11 Serve the Lord with fear,
   and rejoice with trembling.
12 Kiss the Son, lest he be angry,
   and ye perish from the way,
      when his wrath is kindled but a little.

Blessed are all they
that put their trust in him.

3 A psalm of David, when he fled
from Absalom his son.

Lord, how are they increased that trouble me!
Many are they that rise up against me.
² Many there be which say of my soul,
'There is no help for him in God.' Selah.
³ But thou, O Lord, art a shield for me;
my glory, and the lifter up of mine head.
⁴ I cried unto the Lord with my voice,
and he heard me out of his holy hill. Selah.
⁵ I laid me down and slept;
I awaked; for the Lord sustained me.
⁶ I will not be afraid of ten thousands of people,
that have set themselves against me round about.
⁷ Arise, O Lord; save me, O my God,
for thou hast smitten all mine enemies
upon the cheek bone;
thou hast broken the teeth of the ungodly.
⁸ Salvation belongeth unto the Lord:
thy blessing is upon thy people. Selah.

4 To the chief musician on Neginoth,
a psalm of David.

Hear me when I call, O God of my righteousness:

thou hast enlarged me when I was in distress;
have mercy upon me, and hear my prayer.

²O ye sons of men, how long will ye turn
my glory into shame?
How long will ye love vanity,
and seek after leasing? Selah.

³But know that the Lord hath set apart him
that is godly for himself:
the Lord will hear when I call unto him.

⁴Stand in awe, and sin not:
commune with your own heart upon your bed,
and be still. Selah.

⁵Offer the sacrifices of righteousness,
and put your trust in the Lord.

⁶There be many that say,
'Who will shew us any good?
Lord, lift thou up the light
of thy countenance upon us.'

⁷Thou hast put gladness in my heart,
more than in the time that their corn
and their wine increased.

⁸I will both lay me down in peace, and sleep,
for thou, Lord, only makest me dwell in safety.

5 To the chief musician upon Nehiloth,
a psalm of David.

Give ear to my words, O Lord,

consider my meditation.
² Hearken unto the voice of my cry, my King,
    and my God, for unto thee will I pray.
³ My voice shalt thou hear in the morning, O Lord;
    in the morning will I direct my prayer unto thee,
        and will look up.
⁴ For thou art not a God
    that hath pleasure in wickedness;
        neither shall evil dwell with thee.
⁵ The foolish shall not stand in thy sight:
    thou hatest all workers of iniquity.
⁶ Thou shalt destroy them that speak leasing:
    the Lord will abhor the bloody and deceitful man.
⁷ But as for me, I will come into thy house
    in the multitude of thy mercy:
        and in thy fear will I worship
    toward thy holy temple.
⁸ Lead me, O Lord, in thy righteousness
    because of mine enemies;
        make thy way straight before my face.
⁹ For there is no faithfulness in their mouth;
    their inward part is very wickedness;
        their throat is an open sepulchre;
    they flatter with their tongue.
¹⁰ Destroy thou them, O God;
    let them fall by their own counsels;
        cast them out in the multitude
    of their transgressions;

for they have rebelled against thee.
¹¹ But let all those that put their trust in thee rejoice:
  let them ever shout for joy,
    because thou defendest them:
  let them also that love thy name
    be joyful in thee.
¹² For thou, Lord, wilt bless the righteous;
  with favour wilt thou compass him
    as with a shield.

6

To the chief musician on Neginoth upon Sheminith,
  a psalm of David.

O Lord, rebuke me not in thine anger,
  neither chasten me in thy hot displeasure.
² Have mercy upon me,
  O Lord; for I am weak:
    O Lord, heal me; for my bones are vexed.
³ My soul is also sore vexed;
  but thou, O Lord, how long?
⁴ Return, O Lord, deliver my soul:
  oh save me for thy mercies' sake.
⁵ For in death there is no remembrance of thee:
  in the grave who shall give thee thanks?
⁶ I am weary with my groaning;
  all the night make I my bed to swim;
    I water my couch with my tears.
⁷ Mine eye is consumed because of grief;

it waxeth old because of all mine enemies.
⁸ Depart from me, all ye workers of iniquity;
for the Lord hath heard the voice of my weeping.
⁹ The Lord hath heard my supplication;
the Lord will receive my prayer.
¹⁰ Let all mine enemies be ashamed and sore vexed:
let them return and be ashamed suddenly.

7 Shiggaion of David, which he sang unto the Lord,
concerning the words of Cush the Benjamite.

O Lord my God, in thee do I put my trust:
save me from all them that persecute me,
and deliver me,
² lest he tear my soul like a lion, rending it in pieces,
while there is none to deliver.
³ O Lord my God, if I have done this;
if there be iniquity in my hands;
⁴ if I have rewarded evil unto him
that was at peace with me
(yea, I have delivered him
that without cause is mine enemy),
⁵ let the enemy persecute my soul, and take it;
yea, let him tread down my life upon the earth,
and lay mine honour in the dust. Selah.
⁶ Arise, O Lord, in thine anger, lift up thyself
because of the rage of mine enemies:
and awake for me to the judgment
that thou hast commanded.

⁷ So shall the congregation of the people
　　compass thee about:
　　　　for their sakes therefore return thou on high.
⁸ The Lord shall judge the people: judge me, O Lord,
　　according to my righteousness,
　　　　and according to mine integrity that is in me.
⁹ Oh let the wickedness of the wicked come to an end;
　　but establish the just:
　　　　for the righteous God trieth the hearts and reins.
¹⁰ My defence is of God, which saveth
　　the upright in heart.
¹¹ God judgeth the righteous,
　　and God is angry with the wicked every day.
¹² If he turn not, he will whet his sword;
　　he hath bent his bow, and made it ready.
¹³ He hath also prepared for him
　　the instruments of death; he ordaineth his arrows
　　　　against the persecutors.
¹⁴ Behold, he travaileth with iniquity,
　　and hath conceived mischief,
　　　　and brought forth falsehood.
¹⁵ He made a pit, and digged it,
　　and is fallen into the ditch which he made.
¹⁶ His mischief shall return upon his own head,
　　and his violent dealing shall come down
　　　　upon his own pate.
¹⁷ I will praise the Lord
　　according to his righteousness,

and will sing praise to the name
of the Lord most high.

8 To the chief musician upon Gittith,
     a psalm of David.

O Lord our Lord, how excellent is thy name
     in all the earth,
          who hast set thy glory above the heavens!
[2] Out of the mouth of babes and sucklings hast thou
     ordained strength because of thine enemies,
          that thou mightest still the enemy
     and the avenger.
[3] When I consider thy heavens,
     the work of thy fingers, the moon and the stars,
          which thou hast ordained;
[4] what is man, that thou art mindful of him?
     And the son of man, that thou visitest him?
[5] For thou hast made him a little lower
     than the angels,
          and hast crowned him with glory and honour.
[6] Thou madest him to have dominion over
     the works of thy hands;
          thou hast put all things under his feet:
[7] all sheep and oxen, yea,
     and the beasts of the field;
[8] the fowl of the air, and the fish of the sea,
     and whatsoever passeth through
          the paths of the seas.

[9] O Lord our Lord, how excellent is thy name
    in all the earth!

9

To the chief musician upon Muth-labben, a psalm of
    David.

I will praise thee, O Lord, with my whole heart;
    I will shew forth all thy marvellous works.
[2] I will be glad and rejoice in thee:
    I will sing praise to thy name, O thou most High.
[3] When mine enemies are turned back,
    they shall fall and perish at thy presence.
[4] For thou hast maintained my right and my cause;
    thou satest in the throne judging right.
[5] Thou hast rebuked the heathen,
    thou hast destroyed the wicked,
        thou hast put out their name for ever and ever.
[6] O thou enemy, destructions are come
    to a perpetual end: and thou hast destroyed cities;
        their memorial is perished with them.
[7] But the Lord shall endure for ever:
    he hath prepared his throne for judgment.
[8] And he shall judge the world in righteousness,
    he shall minister judgment
        to the people in uprightness.
[9] The Lord also will be a refuge for the oppressed,
    a refuge in times of trouble.

¹⁰And they that know thy name
   will put their trust in thee,
      for thou, Lord, hast not forsaken them
   that seek thee.
¹¹Sing praises to the Lord, which dwelleth in Zion:
   declare among the people his doings.
¹²When he maketh inquisition for blood,
   he remembereth them:
      he forgetteth not the cry of the humble.
¹³Have mercy upon me, O Lord;
   consider my trouble which I suffer
      of them that hate me,
   thou that liftest me up from the gates of death,
¹⁴that I may shew forth all thy praise
   in the gates of the daughter of Zion:
      I will rejoice in thy salvation.
¹⁵The heathen are sunk down
   in the pit that they made:
      in the net which they hid
   is their own foot taken.
¹⁶The Lord is known by the judgment
   which he executeth: the wicked is snared
      in the work of his own hands. Higgaion. Selah.
¹⁷The wicked shall be turned into hell,
   and all the nations that forget God.
¹⁸For the needy shall not alway be forgotten:
   the expectation of the poor
      shall not perish for ever.

¹⁹Arise, O Lord; let not man prevail:
　　let the heathen be judged in thy sight.
²⁰Put them in fear, O Lord:
　　that the nations may know themselves
　　　　to be but men. Selah.

10

Why standest thou afar off, O Lord?
　　Why hidest thou thyself in times of trouble?
²The wicked in his pride doth persecute the poor:
　　let them be taken in the devices
　　　　that they have imagined.
³For the wicked boasteth of his heart's desire,
　　and blesseth the covetous,
　　　　whom the Lord abhorreth.
⁴The wicked, through the pride of his countenance,
　　will not seek after God:
　　　　God is not in all his thoughts.
⁵His ways are always grievous;
　　thy judgments are far above out of his sight:
　　　　as for all his enemies, he puffeth at them.
⁶He hath said in his heart, 'I shall not be moved:
　　for I shall never be in adversity.'
⁷His mouth is full of cursing and deceit and fraud:
　　under his tongue is mischief and vanity.
⁸He sitteth in the lurking places of the villages:
　　in the secret places doth he murder the innocent:
　　　　his eyes are privily set against the poor.

⁹ He lieth in wait secretly as a lion in his den:
    he lieth in wait to catch the poor:
        he doth catch the poor,
    when he draweth him into his net.
¹⁰ He croucheth, and humbleth himself,
    that the poor may fall by his strong ones.
¹¹ He hath said in his heart, God hath forgotten;
    he hideth his face; he will never see it.
¹² Arise, O Lord; O God, lift up thine hand:
    forget not the humble.
¹³ Wherefore doth the wicked contemn God?
    He hath said in his heart,
        'Thou wilt not require it.'
¹⁴ Thou hast seen it;
    for thou beholdest mischief and spite,
        to requite it with thy hand;
    the poor committeth himself unto thee;
        thou art the helper of the fatherless.
¹⁵ Break thou the arm of the wicked and the evil man:
    seek out his wickedness till thou find none.
¹⁶ The Lord is King for ever and ever:
    the heathen are perished out of his land.
¹⁷ Lord, thou hast heard the desire of the humble:
    thou wilt prepare their heart,
        thou wilt cause thine ear to hear:
¹⁸ to judge the fatherless and the oppressed,
    that the man of the earth
        may no more oppress.

11 To the chief musician, a psalm of David.

In the Lord put I my trust: how say ye to my soul,
  'Flee as a bird to your mountain.
² For, lo, the wicked bend their bow,
    they make ready their arrow upon the string,
      that they may privily shoot
    at the upright in heart.
³ If the foundations be destroyed,
    what can the righteous do?'
⁴ The Lord is in his holy temple,
    the Lord's throne is in heaven:
      his eyes behold, his eyelids try,
    the children of men.
⁵ The Lord trieth the righteous; but the wicked
    and him that loveth violence his soul hateth.
⁶ Upon the wicked he shall rain snares,
    fire and brimstone, and an horrible tempest:
      this shall be the portion of their cup.
⁷ For the righteous Lord loveth righteousness;
    his countenance doth behold the upright.

12 To the chief musician upon Sheminith,
    a psalm of David.

Help, Lord; for the godly man ceaseth;
    for the faithful fail from among
      the children of men.

² They speak vanity every one with his neighbour:
    with flattering lips and with a double heart
        do they speak.
³ The Lord shall cut off all flattering lips,
    and the tongue that speaketh proud things:
⁴ who have said, 'With our tongue will we prevail;
    our lips are our own: who is lord over us?'
⁵ 'For the oppression of the poor,
    for the sighing of the needy,
        now will I arise,' saith the Lord;
    I will set him in safety from him
        that puffeth at him.
⁶ The words of the Lord are pure words:
    as silver tried in a furnace of earth,
        purified seven times.
⁷ Thou shalt keep them, O Lord,
    thou shalt preserve them
        from this generation for ever.
⁸ The wicked walk on every side,
    when the vilest men are exalted.

13 To the chief musician, a psalm of David.

How long wilt thou forget me,
    O Lord? For ever?
        How long wilt thou hide
    thy face from me?
² How long shall I take counsel in my soul,
    having sorrow in my heart daily?

How long shall mine enemy
be exalted over me?
3 Consider and hear me, O Lord my God:
lighten mine eyes, lest I sleep the sleep of death;
4 lest mine enemy say,
'I have prevailed against him';
and those that trouble me rejoice
when I am moved.
5 But I have trusted in thy mercy;
my heart shall rejoice in thy salvation.
6 I will sing unto the Lord,
because he hath dealt bountifully with me.

14

To the chief musician, a psalm of David.

The fool hath said in his heart, 'There is no God.'
They are corrupt, they have done
abominable works,
there is none that doeth good.
2 The Lord looked down from heaven
upon the children of men, to see if there were
any that did understand, and seek God.
3 They are all gone aside, they are all together
become filthy: there is none that doeth good,
no, not one.
4 Have all the workers of iniquity no knowledge?
Who eat up my people as they eat bread,
and call not upon the Lord.

⁵ There were they in great fear:
    for God is in the generation of the righteous.
⁶ Ye have shamed the counsel of the poor,
    because the Lord is his refuge.
⁷ Oh that the salvation of Israel
    were come out of Zion!
        When the Lord bringeth back
    the captivity of his people,
        Jacob shall rejoice, and Israel shall be glad.

15

A psalm of David.

Lord, who shall abide in thy tabernacle?
    Who shall dwell in thy holy hill?
² He that walketh uprightly,
    and worketh righteousness,
        and speaketh the truth in his heart.
³ He that backbiteth not with his tongue,
    nor doeth evil to his neighbour, nor taketh up
    a reproach against his neighbour.
⁴ In whose eyes a vile person is contemned;
    but he honoureth them that fear the Lord.
        He that sweareth to his own hurt,
    and changeth not.
⁵ He that putteth not out his money to usury,
    nor taketh reward against the innocent.
        He that doeth these things
    shall never be moved.

16

Michtam of David.

Preserve me, O God, for in thee
    do I put my trust.
² O my soul, thou hast said unto the Lord
      'Thou art my Lord: my goodness extendeth
          not to thee,
³ but to the saints that are in the earth,
    and to the excellent,
        in whom is all my delight.'
⁴ Their sorrows shall be multiplied
    that hasten after another god:
        their drink offerings of blood will I not offer,
    nor take up their names into my lips.
⁵ The Lord is the portion of mine inheritance
    and of my cup: thou maintainest my lot.
⁶ The lines are fallen unto me in pleasant places;
    yea, I have a goodly heritage.
⁷ I will bless the Lord, who hath given me counsel:
    my reins also instruct me in the night seasons.
⁸ I have set the Lord always before me:
    because he is at my right hand,
        I shall not be moved.
⁹ Therefore my heart is glad, and my glory rejoiceth:
    my flesh also shall rest in hope.
¹⁰ For thou wilt not leave my soul in hell;
    neither wilt thou suffer thine Holy One
        to see corruption.

11 Thou wilt shew me the path of life:
    in thy presence is fulness of joy;
        at thy right hand there are pleasures
    for evermore.

17

A prayer of David.

Hear the right, O Lord, attend unto my cry,
    give ear unto my prayer,
        that goeth not out of feigned lips.
2 Let my sentence come forth from thy presence;
    let thine eyes behold
        the things that are equal.
3 Thou hast proved mine heart;
    thou hast visited me in the night;
        thou hast tried me, and shalt find nothing;
    I am purposed that my mouth
        shall not transgress.
4 Concerning the works of men,
    by the word of thy lips I have kept me
        from the paths of the destroyer.
5 Hold up my goings in thy paths,
    that my footsteps slip not.
6 I have called upon thee, for thou wilt hear me,
    O God: incline thine ear unto me,
        and hear my speech.
7 Shew thy marvellous lovingkindness,
    O thou that savest by thy right hand

them which put their trust in thee
from those that rise up against them.

⁸ Keep me as the apple of the eye,
hide me under the shadow of thy wings,
⁹ from the wicked that oppress me,
from my deadly enemies,
who compass me about.
¹⁰ They are inclosed in their own fat:
with their mouth they speak proudly.
¹¹ They have now compassed us in our steps:
they have set their eyes bowing down
to the earth,
¹² like as a lion that is greedy of his prey,
and as it were a young lion
lurking in secret places.
¹³ Arise, O Lord, disappoint him, cast him down:
deliver my soul from the wicked,
which is thy sword:
¹⁴ from men which are thy hand, O Lord,
from men of the world,
which have their portion in this life,
and whose belly thou fillest
with thy hid treasure: they are full of children,
and leave the rest of their substance
to their babes.
¹⁵ As for me, I will behold thy face in righteousness:
I shall be satisfied, when I awake,
with thy likeness.

18 To the chief musician, a psalm of David, the servant
of the Lord, who spake unto the Lord the words
of this song in the day that the Lord delivered
him from the hand of all his enemies, and from
the hand of Saul: and he said,

I will love thee, O Lord, my strength.
² The Lord is my rock, and my fortress,
and my deliverer;
my God, my strength, in whom I will trust;
my buckler, and the horn of my salvation,
and my high tower.
³ I will call upon the Lord, who is worthy
to be praised:
so shall I be saved from mine enemies.
⁴ The sorrows of death compassed me,
and the floods of ungodly men made me afraid.
⁵ The sorrows of hell compassed me
about: the snares of death prevented me.
⁶ In my distress I called upon the Lord,
and cried unto my God:
he heard my voice out of his temple,
and my cry came before him, even into his ears.
⁷ Then the earth shook and trembled;
the foundations also of the hills moved
and were shaken, because he was wroth.
⁸ There went up a smoke out of his nostrils,
and fire out of his mouth devoured:
coals were kindled by it.

⁹He bowed the heavens also, and came down:
  and darkness was under his feet.
¹⁰And he rode upon a cherub, and did fly:
  yea, he did fly upon the wings of the wind.
¹¹He made darkness his secret place;
  his pavilion round about him were dark waters
    and thick clouds of the skies.
¹²At the brightness that was before him
  his thick clouds passed,
    hail stones and coals of fire.
¹³The Lord also thundered in the heavens,
  and the Highest gave his voice;
    hail stones and coals of fire.
¹⁴Yea, he sent out his arrows, and scattered them;
  and he shot out lightnings,
    and discomfited them.
¹⁵Then the channels of waters were seen,
  and the foundations of the world
    were discovered at thy rebuke, O Lord,
  at the blast of the breath of thy nostrils.
¹⁶He sent from above, he took me,
  he drew me out of many waters.
¹⁷He delivered me from my strong enemy,
  and from them which hated me:
    for they were too strong for me.
¹⁸They prevented me in the day of my calamity;
  but the Lord was my stay.
¹⁹He brought me forth also into a large place;

he delivered me, because he delighted in me.
²⁰ The Lord rewarded me
according to my righteousness;
according to the cleanness of my hands
hath he recompensed me.
²¹ For I have kept the ways of the Lord,
and have not wickedly departed from my God.
²² For all his judgments were before me,
and I did not put away his statutes from me.
²³ I was also upright before him,
and I kept myself from mine iniquity.
²⁴ Therefore hath the Lord recompensed me
according to my righteousness,
according to the cleanness of my hands
in his eyesight.
²⁵ With the merciful thou wilt shew thyself merciful;
with an upright man
thou wilt shew thyself upright;
²⁶ with the pure thou wilt shew thyself pure;
and with the froward
thou wilt shew thyself froward.
²⁷ For thou wilt save the afflicted people;
but wilt bring down high looks.
²⁸ For thou wilt light my candle:
the Lord my God will enlighten my darkness.
²⁹ For by thee I have run through a troop;
and by my God have I leaped over a wall.
³⁰ As for God, his way is perfect:

the word of the Lord is tried:

> he is a buckler to all those that trust in him.

³¹ For who is God save the Lord?

> Or who is a rock save our God?

³² It is God that girdeth me with strength,

> and maketh my way perfect.

³³ He maketh my feet like hinds' feet,

> and setteth me upon my high places.

³⁴ He teacheth my hands to war,

> so that a bow of steel is broken by mine arms.

³⁵ Thou hast also given me the shield of thy salvation:

> and thy right hand hath holden me up,
>> and thy gentleness hath made me great.

³⁶ Thou hast enlarged my steps under me,

> that my feet did not slip.

³⁷ I have pursued mine enemies, and overtaken them:

> neither did I turn again till they were consumed.

³⁸ I have wounded them that they were not able

> to rise: they are fallen under my feet.

³⁹ For thou hast girded me with strength

> unto the battle: thou hast subdued under me
>> those that rose up against me.

⁴⁰ Thou hast also given me the necks of mine enemies;

> that I might destroy them that hate me.

⁴¹ They cried, but there was none to save them:

> even unto the Lord, but he answered them not.

⁴² Then did I beat them small as the dust

> before the wind:

I did cast them out as the dirt in the streets.
⁴³ Thou hast delivered me
from the strivings of the people;
and thou hast made me
the head of the heathen: a people whom
I have not known shall serve me.
⁴⁴ As soon as they hear of me, they shall obey me:
the strangers shall submit themselves unto me.
⁴⁵ The strangers shall fade away,
and be afraid out of their close places.
⁴⁶ The Lord liveth; and blessed be my rock;
and let the God of my salvation be exalted.
⁴⁷ It is God that avengeth me,
and subdueth the people under me.
⁴⁸ He delivereth me from mine enemies:
yea, thou liftest me up above
those that rise up against me:
thou hast delivered me from the violent man.
⁴⁹ Therefore will I give thanks unto thee,
O Lord, among the heathen,
and sing praises unto thy name.
⁵⁰ Great deliverance giveth he to his king;
and sheweth mercy to his anointed, to David,
and to his seed for evermore.

19

To the chief musician, a psalm of David.

The heavens declare the glory of God;

and the firmament sheweth his handywork.
² Day unto day uttereth speech,
and night unto night sheweth knowledge.
³ There is no speech nor language,
where their voice is not heard.
⁴ Their line is gone out through all the earth,
and their words to the end of the world.
In them hath he set a tabernacle for the sun,
⁵ which is as a bridegroom
coming out of his chamber,
and rejoiceth as a strong man to run a race.
⁶ His going forth is from the end of the heaven,
and his circuit unto the ends of it;
and there is nothing hid
from the heat thereof.
⁷ The law of the Lord is perfect, converting the soul:
the testimony of the Lord is sure,
making wise the simple.
⁸ The statutes of the Lord are right,
rejoicing the heart:
the commandment of the Lord is pure,
enlightening the eyes.
⁹ The fear of the Lord is clean, enduring for ever:
the judgments of the Lord are true
and righteous altogether.
¹⁰ More to be desired are they than gold,
yea, than much fine gold:
sweeter also than honey and the honeycomb.

¹¹ Moreover by them is thy servant warned;
   and in keeping of them there is great reward.
¹² Who can understand his errors?
   Cleanse thou me from secret faults.
¹³ Keep back thy servant also
   from presumptuous sins;
      let them not have dominion over me:
      then shall I be upright, and I shall be innocent
      from the great transgression.
¹⁴ Let the words of my mouth,
   and the meditation of my heart,
      be acceptable in thy sight, O Lord,
      my strength, and my redeemer.

20

To the chief musician, a psalm of David.

The Lord hear thee in the day of trouble;
   the name of the God of Jacob defend thee;
² send thee help from the sanctuary,
   and strengthen thee out of Zion;
³ remember all thy offerings,
   and accept thy burnt sacrifice; Selah.
⁴ Grant thee according to thine own heart,
   and fulfil all thy counsel.
⁵ We will rejoice in thy salvation,
   and in the name of our God
      we will set up our banners:
      the Lord fulfil all thy petitions.

⁶ Now know I that the Lord saveth his anointed;
  he will hear him from his holy heaven with the
    saving strength of his right hand.
⁷ Some trust in chariots, and some in horses;
  but we will remember the name
    of the Lord our God.
⁸ They are brought down and fallen;
  but we are risen, and stand upright.
⁹ Save, Lord: let the king hear us when we call.

21

To the chief musician, a psalm of David.

The king shall joy in thy strength, O Lord;
  and in thy salvation how greatly shall he rejoice!
² Thou hast given him his heart's desire, and hast not
  withholden the request of his lips. Selah.
³ For thou preventest him
  with the blessings of goodness:
    thou settest a crown of pure gold on his head.
⁴ He asked life of thee, and thou gavest it him,
  even length of days for ever and ever.
⁵ His glory is great in thy salvation:
  honour and majesty hast thou laid upon him.
⁶ For thou hast made him most blessed for ever:
  thou hast made him exceeding glad
    with thy countenance.
⁷ For the king trusteth in the Lord,
  and through the mercy of the most High
    he shall not be moved.

⁸ Thine hand shall find out all thine enemies:
    thy right hand shall find out those that hate thee.
⁹ Thou shalt make them as a fiery oven
    in the time of thine anger:
        the Lord shall swallow them up in his wrath,
        and the fire shall devour them.
¹⁰ Their fruit shalt thou destroy from the earth,
    and their seed from among the children of men.
¹¹ For they intended evil against thee:
    they imagined a mischievous device,
        which they are not able to perform.
¹² Therefore shalt thou make them turn their back,
    when thou shalt make ready thine arrows
        upon thy strings against the face of them.
¹³ Be thou exalted, Lord, in thine own strength:
    so will we sing and praise thy power.

22

To the chief musician upon Aijeleth Shahar,
    a psalm of David.

My God, my God, why hast thou forsaken me?
    Why art thou so far from helping me,
        and from the words of my roaring?
² O my God, I cry in the daytime,
    but thou hearest not;
        and in the night season, and am not silent.
³ But thou art holy,
    O thou that inhabitest the praises of Israel.

⁴ Our fathers trusted in thee:
    they trusted, and thou didst deliver them.
⁵ They cried unto thee, and were delivered:
    they trusted in thee, and were not confounded.
⁶ But I am a worm, and no man;
    a reproach of men, and despised of the people.
⁷ All they that see me laugh me to scorn:
    they shoot out the lip,
        they shake the head, saying,
⁸ 'He trusted on the Lord that he would deliver him:
    let him deliver him,
        seeing he delighted in him.'
⁹ But thou art he that took me out of the womb:
    thou didst make me hope when I was upon
        my mother's breasts.
¹⁰ I was cast upon thee from the womb:
    thou art my God from my mother's belly.
¹¹ Be not far from me;
    for trouble is near;
        for there is none to help.
¹² Many bulls have compassed me:
    strong bulls of Bashan have beset me round.
¹³ They gaped upon me with their mouths,
    as a ravening and a roaring lion.
¹⁴ I am poured out like water,
    and all my bones are out of joint:
        my heart is like wax; it is melted
        in the midst of my bowels.

¹⁵ My strength is dried up like a potsherd;
   and my tongue cleaveth to my jaws;
      and thou hast brought me
   into the dust of death.
¹⁶ For dogs have compassed me:
   the assembly of the wicked have inclosed me:
      they pierced my hands and my feet.
¹⁷ I may tell all my bones:
   they look and stare upon me.
¹⁸ They part my garments among them,
   and cast lots upon my vesture.
¹⁹ But be not thou far from me, O Lord:
   O my strength, haste thee to help me.
²⁰ Deliver my soul from the sword;
   my darling from the power of the dog.
²¹ Save me from the lion's mouth,
   for thou hast heard me from the horns
      of the unicorns.
²² I will declare thy name unto my brethren:
   in the midst of the congregation
      will I praise thee.
²³ Ye that fear the Lord, praise him;
   all ye the seed of Jacob, glorify him;
      and fear him, all ye the seed of Israel.
²⁴ For he hath not despised nor abhorred
   the affliction of the afflicted;
      neither hath he hid his face from him;
   but when he cried unto him, he heard.

²⁵ My praise shall be of thee
　　in the great congregation:
　　　　I will pay my vows before them
　　that fear him.
²⁶ The meek shall eat and be satisfied:
　　they shall praise the Lord that seek him:
　　　　your heart shall live for ever.
²⁷All the ends of the world shall remember
　　and turn unto the Lord:
　　　　and all the kindreds of the nations
　　shall worship before thee.
²⁸ For the kingdom is the Lord's:
　　and he is the governor among the nations.
²⁹All they that be fat upon earth shall eat
　　and worship: all they that go down to the dust
　　　　shall bow before him:
　　and none can keep alive his own soul.
³⁰A seed shall serve him; it shall be accounted
　　to the Lord for a generation.
³¹ They shall come, and shall declare
　　his righteousness unto a people
　　　　that shall be born, that he hath done this.

23

A psalm of David.

The Lord is my shepherd; I shall not want.
² He maketh me to lie down in green pastures:
　　he leadeth me beside the still waters.

³ He restoreth my soul:
    he leadeth me in the paths of righteousness
        for his name's sake.
⁴ Yea, though I walk
    through the valley of
        the shadow of death,
    I will fear no evil;
        for thou art with me;
    thy rod and thy staff they comfort me.
⁵ Thou preparest a table before me
    in the presence of mine enemies;
        thou anointest my head with oil;
    my cup runneth over.
⁶ Surely goodness and mercy shall follow me
    all the days of my life;
        and I will dwell
    in the house of the Lord for ever.

24 A psalm of David.

The earth is the Lord's, and the fulness thereof;
    the world, and they that dwell therein.
² For he hath founded it upon the seas,
    and established it upon the floods.
³ Who shall ascend into the hill of the Lord?
    Or who shall stand in his holy place?
⁴ He that hath clean hands, and a pure heart;
    who hath not lifted up his soul unto vanity,
        nor sworn deceitfully.

⁵ He shall receive the blessing from the Lord,
  and righteousness from the God
    of his salvation.
⁶ This is the generation of them that seek him,
  that seek thy face, O Jacob. Selah.
⁷ Lift up your heads, O ye gates;
  and be ye lift up, ye everlasting doors;
    and the King of glory shall come in.
⁸ Who is this King of glory?
  The Lord strong and mighty,
    the Lord mighty in battle.
⁹ Lift up your heads, O ye gates;
  even lift them up, ye everlasting doors;
    and the King of glory shall come in.
¹⁰ Who is this King of glory?
  The Lord of hosts, he is the King of glory. Selah.

25

A psalm of David.

Unto thee, O Lord, do I lift up my soul.
² O my God, I trust in thee: let me not be ashamed,
  let not mine enemies triumph over me.
³ Yea, let none that wait on thee be ashamed:
  let them be ashamed
    which transgress without cause.
⁴ Shew me thy ways, O Lord;
  teach me thy paths.

⁵ Lead me in thy truth, and teach me:
>   for thou art the God of my salvation;
>   on thee do I wait all the day.

⁶ Remember, O Lord,
>   thy tender mercies and thy lovingkindnesses;
>   for they have been ever of old.

⁷ Remember not the sins of my youth,
>   nor my transgressions:
>   according to thy mercy, remember thou me
>   for thy goodness' sake, O Lord.

⁸ Good and upright is the Lord;
>   therefore will he teach sinners in the way.

⁹ The meek will he guide in judgment;
>   and the meek will he teach his way.

¹⁰ All the paths of the Lord are mercy and truth
>   unto such as keep his covenant
>   and his testimonies.

¹¹ For thy name's sake, O Lord,
>   pardon mine iniquity; for it is great.

¹² What man is he that feareth the Lord?
>   Him shall he teach in the way
>   that he shall choose.

¹³ His soul shall dwell at ease;
>   and his seed shall inherit the earth.

¹⁴ The secret of the Lord is with them that fear him;
>   and he will shew them his covenant.

¹⁵ Mine eyes are ever toward the Lord;
>   for he shall pluck my feet out of the net.

[16] Turn thee unto me, and have mercy upon me;
    for I am desolate and afflicted.
[17] The troubles of my heart are enlarged:
    O bring thou me out of my distresses.
[18] Look upon mine affliction and my pain;
    and forgive all my sins.
[19] Consider mine enemies; for they are many;
    and they hate me with cruel hatred.
[20] O keep my soul, and deliver me:
    let me not be ashamed;
        for I put my trust in thee.
[21] Let integrity and uprightness preserve me;
    for I wait on thee.
[22] Redeem Israel, O God, out of all his troubles.

26

A psalm of David.

Judge me, O Lord; for I have walked in mine integrity:
    I have trusted also in the Lord;
        therefore I shall not slide.
[2] Examine me, O Lord, and prove me;
    try my reins and my heart.
[3] For thy lovingkindness is before mine eyes:
    and I have walked in thy truth.
[4] I have not sat with vain persons,
    neither will I go in with dissemblers.
[5] I have hated the congregation of evil doers;
    and will not sit with the wicked.

⁶ I will wash mine hands in innocency:
    so will I compass thine altar, O Lord,
⁷ that I may publish with the voice of thanksgiving,
    and tell of all thy wondrous works.
⁸ Lord, I have loved the habitation of thy house,
    and the place where thine honour dwelleth.
⁹ Gather not my soul with sinners,
    nor my life with bloody men,
¹⁰ In whose hands is mischief,
    and their right hand is full of bribes.
¹¹ But as for me, I will walk in mine integrity:
    redeem me, and be merciful unto me.
¹² My foot standeth in an even place:
    in the congregations will I bless the Lord.

27

A psalm of David.

The Lord is my light and my salvation;
    whom shall I fear?
        The Lord is the strength of my life;
    of whom shall I be afraid?
² When the wicked, even mine enemies and my foes,
    came upon me to eat up my flesh,
        they stumbled and fell.
³ Though an host should encamp against me,
    my heart shall not fear:
        though war should rise against me,
    in this will I be confident.

⁴ One thing have I desired of the Lord,
    that will I seek after;
        that I may dwell in the house of the Lord
    all the days of my life,
        to behold the beauty of the Lord,
    and to enquire in his temple.
⁵ For in the time of trouble he shall hide me
    in his pavilion:
        in the secret of his tabernacle
    shall he hide me;
        he shall set me up upon a rock.
⁶ And now shall mine head be lifted up
    above mine enemies round about me:
        therefore will I offer in his tabernacle
    sacrifices of joy; I will sing,
        yea, I will sing praises unto the Lord.
⁷ Hear, O Lord, when I cry with my voice:
    have mercy also upon me, and answer me.
⁸ When thou saidst, 'Seek ye my face',
    my heart said unto thee,
        'Thy face, Lord, will I seek.'
⁹ Hide not thy face far from me;
    put not thy servant away in anger:
        thou hast been my help;
    leave me not, neither forsake me,
        O God of my salvation.
¹⁰ When my father and my mother forsake me,
    then the Lord will take me up.

¹¹ Teach me thy way, O Lord,
>> and lead me in a plain path,
>>> because of mine enemies.
¹² Deliver me not over unto the will of mine enemies:
>> for false witnesses are risen up against me,
>>> and such as breathe out cruelty.
¹³ I had fainted, unless I had believed
>> to see the goodness of the Lord
>>> in the land of the living.
¹⁴ Wait on the Lord: be of good courage,
>> and he shall strengthen thine heart:
>>> wait, I say, on the Lord.

28

A psalm of David.

Unto thee will I cry, O Lord my rock;
>> be not silent to me:
>>> lest, if thou be silent to me,
>> I become like them
>>> that go down into the pit.
² Hear the voice of my supplications,
>> when I cry unto thee,
>>> when I lift up my hands toward thy holy oracle.
³ Draw me not away with the wicked,
>> and with the workers of iniquity,
>>> which speak peace to their neighbours,
>> but mischief is in their hearts.

⁴ Give them according to their deeds,
    and according to the wickedness
        of their endeavours;
    give them after the work of their hands;
        render to them their desert.
⁵ Because they regard not the works of the Lord,
    nor the operation of his hands,
        he shall destroy them, and not build them up.
⁶ Blessed be the Lord, because he hath heard
    the voice of my supplications.
⁷ The Lord is my strength and my shield;
    my heart trusted in him, and I am helped:
        therefore my heart greatly rejoiceth;
    and with my song will I praise him.
⁸ The Lord is their strength, and he is the saving
    strength of his anointed.
⁹ Save thy people, and bless thine inheritance:
    feed them also, and lift them up for ever.

29 A psalm of David.

Give unto the Lord, O ye mighty,
    give unto the Lord glory and strength.
² Give unto the Lord the glory due unto his name;
    worship the Lord in the beauty of holiness.
³ The voice of the Lord is upon the waters:
    the God of glory thundereth:
        the Lord is upon many waters.

⁴The voice of the Lord is powerful;
   the voice of the Lord is full of majesty.
⁵The voice of the Lord breaketh the cedars;
   yea, the Lord breaketh the cedars of Lebanon.
⁶He maketh them also to skip like a calf;
   Lebanon and Sirion like a young unicorn.
⁷The voice of the Lord divideth the flames of fire.
⁸The voice of the Lord shaketh the wilderness;
   the Lord shaketh the wilderness of Kadesh.
⁹The voice of the Lord maketh the hinds to calve,
   and discovereth the forests:
      and in his temple doth every one speak
   of his glory.
¹⁰The Lord sitteth upon the flood;
   yea, the Lord sitteth King for ever.
¹¹The Lord will give strength unto his people;
   the Lord will bless his people with peace.

30 A psalm and song at the dedication of the house
   of David.

I will extol thee, O Lord;
   for thou hast lifted me up,
      and hast not made my foes to rejoice over me.
²O Lord my God, I cried unto thee,
   and thou hast healed me.
³O Lord, thou hast brought up my soul
   from the grave: thou hast kept me alive,
      that I should not go down to the pit.

⁴ Sing unto the Lord, O ye saints of his,
    and give thanks at the remembrance
        of his holiness.
⁵ For his anger endureth but a moment;
    in his favour is life:
        weeping may endure for a night,
    but joy cometh in the morning.
⁶ And in my prosperity I said,
    'I shall never be moved.'
⁷ Lord, by thy favour thou hast made my mountain
    to stand strong: thou didst hide thy face,
        and I was troubled.
⁸ I cried to thee, O Lord;
    and unto the Lord I made supplication.
⁹ What profit is there in my blood,
    when I go down to the pit?
        Shall the dust praise thee?
        Shall it declare thy truth?
¹⁰ Hear, O Lord, and have mercy upon me:
    Lord, be thou my helper.
¹¹ Thou hast turned for me my mourning
    into dancing:
        thou hast put off my sackcloth,
    and girded me with gladness;
¹² to the end that my glory may sing praise to thee,
    and not be silent.
        O Lord my God,
    I will give thanks unto thee for ever.

31

To the chief musician, a psalm of David.

In thee, O Lord, do I put my trust;
  let me never be ashamed;
    deliver me in thy righteousness.
2 Bow down thine ear to me;
  deliver me speedily:
    be thou my strong rock,
  for an house of defence to save me.
3 For thou art my rock and my fortress;
  therefore for thy name's sake lead me,
    and guide me.
4 Pull me out of the net that they have laid
  privily for me; for thou art my strength.
5 Into thine hand I commit my spirit:
  thou hast redeemed me,
    O Lord God of truth.
6 I have hated them that regard lying vanities;
  but I trust in the Lord.
7 I will be glad and rejoice in thy mercy;
  for thou hast considered my trouble;
    thou hast known my soul in adversities,
8 and hast not shut me up into the hand of the enemy:
  thou hast set my feet in a large room.
9 Have mercy upon me, O Lord,
  for I am in trouble:
    mine eye is consumed with grief,
  yea, my soul and my belly.

¹⁰ For my life is spent with grief,
   and my years with sighing:
      my strength faileth because of mine iniquity,
      and my bones are consumed.
¹¹ I was a reproach among all mine enemies,
   but especially among my neighbours,
      and a fear to mine acquaintance:
      they that did see me without fled from me.
¹² I am forgotten as a dead man out of mind:
   I am like a broken vessel.
¹³ For I have heard the slander of many:
   fear was on every side:
      while they took counsel together against me,
      they devised to take away my life.
¹⁴ But I trusted in thee, O Lord:
   I said, 'Thou art my God.'
¹⁵ My times are in thy hand:
   deliver me from the hand of mine enemies,
      and from them that persecute me.
¹⁶ Make thy face to shine upon thy servant:
   save me for thy mercies' sake.
¹⁷ Let me not be ashamed, O Lord;
   for I have called upon thee:
      let the wicked be ashamed,
      and let them be silent in the grave.
¹⁸ Let the lying lips be put to silence,
   which speak grievous things proudly
      and contemptuously against the righteous.

¹⁹ Oh how great is thy goodness,
   which thou hast laid up for them that fear thee;
      which thou hast wrought for them
      that trust in thee before the sons of men!
²⁰ Thou shalt hide them in the secret of thy presence
   from the pride of man:
      thou shalt keep them secretly in a pavilion
      from the strife of tongues.
²¹ Blessed be the Lord;
   for he hath shewed me his marvellous kindness
      in a strong city.
²² For I said in my haste,
   'I am cut off from before thine eyes':
      nevertheless thou heardest the voice
      of my supplications when I cried unto thee.
²³ O love the Lord, all ye his saints;
   for the Lord preserveth the faithful,
      and plentifully rewardeth the proud doer.
²⁴ Be of good courage, and he shall strengthen
   your heart, all ye that hope in the Lord.

32 A psalm of David, Maschil.

Blessed is he whose transgression is forgiven,
   whose sin is covered.
² Blessed is the man unto whom
   the Lord imputeth not iniquity,
      and in whose spirit there is no guile.

³ When I kept silence, my bones waxed old
through my roaring all the day long.
⁴ For day and night thy hand was heavy upon me:
my moisture is turned
into the drought of summer. Selah.
⁵ I acknowledged my sin unto thee,
and mine iniquity have I not hid.
I said, 'I will confess my transgressions
unto the Lord'; and thou forgavest the iniquity
of my sin. Selah.
⁶ For this shall every one that is godly pray
unto thee in a time when thou mayest be found:
surely in the floods of great waters
they shall not come nigh unto him.
⁷ Thou art my hiding place;
thou shalt preserve me from trouble;
thou shalt compass me about
with songs of deliverance. Selah.
⁸ I will instruct thee and teach thee in the way
which thou shalt go:
I will guide thee with mine eye.
⁹ Be ye not as the horse, or as the mule,
which have no understanding:
whose mouth must be held in with bit
and bridle, lest they come near unto thee.
¹⁰ Many sorrows shall be to the wicked:
but he that trusteth in the Lord,
mercy shall compass him about.

¹¹Be glad in the Lord, and rejoice, ye righteous:
>   and shout for joy, all ye that are upright in heart.

33

Rejoice in the Lord, O ye righteous;
>   for praise is comely for the upright.

²Praise the Lord with harp:
>   sing unto him with the psaltery
>   and an instrument of ten strings.

³Sing unto him a new song;
>   play skilfully with a loud noise.

⁴For the word of the Lord is right;
>   and all his works are done in truth.

⁵He loveth righteousness and judgment:
>   the earth is full of the goodness of the Lord.

⁶By the word of the Lord were the heavens made;
>   and all the host of them
>   by the breath of his mouth.

⁷He gathereth the waters of the sea together
>   as an heap:
>   he layeth up the depth in storehouses.

⁸Let all the earth fear the Lord:
>   let all the inhabitants of the world
>   stand in awe of him.

⁹For he spake, and it was done;
>   he commanded, and it stood fast.

¹⁰The Lord bringeth the counsel of the heathen
>   to nought:
>   he maketh the devices of the people
>   of none effect.

¹¹ The counsel of the Lord standeth for ever,
   the thoughts of his heart to all generations.
¹² Blessed is the nation whose God is the Lord;
   and the people whom he hath chosen
      for his own inheritance.
¹³ The Lord looketh from heaven;
   he beholdeth all the sons of men.
¹⁴ From the place of his habitation
   he looketh upon all the inhabitants of the earth.
¹⁵ He fashioneth their hearts alike;
   he considereth all their works.
¹⁶ There is no king saved
   by the multitude of an host:
      a mighty man
   is not delivered by much strength.
¹⁷ An horse is a vain thing for safety:
   neither shall he deliver any
      by his great strength.
¹⁸ Behold, the eye of the Lord is upon them that
   fear him, upon them that hope in his mercy;
¹⁹ to deliver their soul from death,
   and to keep them alive in famine.
²⁰ Our soul waiteth for the Lord:
   he is our help and our shield.
²¹ For our heart shall rejoice in him,
   because we have trusted in his holy name.
²² Let thy mercy, O Lord,
   be upon us, according as we hope in thee.

34

A psalm of David, when he changed his behaviour
before Abimelech, who drove him away,
and he departed.

I will bless the Lord at all times:
　　his praise shall continually be in my mouth.
2 My soul shall make her boast in the Lord:
　　the humble shall hear thereof, and be glad.
3 O magnify the Lord with me,
　　and let us exalt his name together.
4 I sought the Lord, and he heard me,
　　and delivered me from all my fears.
5 They looked unto him, and were lightened:
　　and their faces were not ashamed.
6 This poor man cried, and the Lord heard him,
　　and saved him out of all his troubles.
7 The angel of the Lord encampeth round about
　　them that fear him, and delivereth them.
8 O taste and see that the Lord is good:
　　blessed is the man that trusteth in him.
9 O fear the Lord, ye his saints;
　　for there is no want to them that fear him.
10 The young lions do lack, and suffer hunger;
　　but they that seek the Lord shall not want
　　　　any good thing.
11 Come, ye children, hearken unto me:
　　I will teach you the fear of the Lord.
12 What man is he that desireth life,
　　and loveth many days, that he may see good?

¹³ Keep thy tongue from evil,
   and thy lips from speaking guile.
¹⁴ Depart from evil, and do good;
   seek peace, and pursue it.
¹⁵ The eyes of the Lord are upon the righteous,
   and his ears are open unto their cry.
¹⁶ The face of the Lord is against them that do evil,
   to cut off the remembrance of them
      from the earth.
¹⁷ The righteous cry, and the Lord heareth,
   and delivereth them out of all their troubles.
¹⁸ The Lord is nigh unto them
   that are of a broken heart;
      and saveth such as be of a contrite spirit.
¹⁹ Many are the afflictions of the righteous;
   but the Lord delivereth him out of them all.
²⁰ He keepeth all his bones:
   not one of them is broken.
²¹ Evil shall slay the wicked:
   and they that hate the righteous shall be desolate.
²² The Lord redeemeth the soul of his servants:
   and none of them that trust in him
      shall be desolate.

35 A psalm of David.

Plead my cause, O Lord,
   with them that strive with me:
      fight against them that fight against me.

² Take hold of shield and buckler,
and stand up for mine help.
³ Draw out also the spear, and stop the way
against them that persecute me:
say unto my soul, 'I am thy salvation.'
⁴ Let them be confounded and put to shame
that seek after my soul:
let them be turned back
and brought to confusion that devise my hurt.
⁵ Let them be as chaff before the wind;
and let the angel of the Lord chase them.
⁶ Let their way be dark and slippery;
and let the angel of the Lord persecute them.
⁷ For without cause have they hid for me their net
in a pit, which without cause
they have digged for my soul.
⁸ Let destruction come upon him at unawares;
and let his net that he hath hid catch himself:
into that very destruction let him fall.
⁹ And my soul shall be joyful in the Lord:
it shall rejoice in his salvation.
¹⁰ All my bones shall say, 'Lord, who is like unto thee,
which deliverest the poor from him
that is too strong for him,
yea, the poor and the needy from him
that spoileth him?'
¹¹ False witnesses did rise up;
they laid to my charge things that I knew not.

¹² They rewarded me evil for good
     to the spoiling of my soul.
¹³ But as for me, when they were sick,
     my clothing was sackcloth:
          I humbled my soul with fasting;
     and my prayer returned into mine own bosom.
¹⁴ I behaved myself as though he had been my friend
     or brother: I bowed down heavily,
          as one that mourneth for his mother.
¹⁵ But in mine adversity they rejoiced,
     and gathered themselves together:
          yea, the abjects gathered themselves together
     against me, and I knew it not;
          they did tear me, and ceased not:
¹⁶ with hypocritical mockers in feasts,
     they gnashed upon me with their teeth.
¹⁷ Lord, how long wilt thou look on?
     Rescue my soul from their destructions,
          my darling from the lions.
¹⁸ I will give thee thanks in the great congregation:
     I will praise thee among much people.
¹⁹ Let not them that are mine enemies
     wrongfully rejoice over me:
          neither let them wink with the eye
     that hate me without a cause.
²⁰ For they speak not peace: but they devise
     deceitful matters against them
          that are quiet in the land.
²¹ Yea, they opened their mouth wide against me,

and said, 'Aha, aha, our eye hath seen it.'

²² This thou hast seen, O Lord: keep not silence:
O Lord, be not far from me.

²³ Stir up thyself, and awake to my judgment,
even unto my cause, my God and my Lord.

²⁴ Judge me, O Lord my God,
according to thy righteousness;
and let them not rejoice over me.

²⁵ Let them not say in their hearts,
'Ah, so would we have it': let them not say,
'We have swallowed him up.'

²⁶ Let them be ashamed and brought to confusion
together that rejoice at mine hurt:
let them be clothed with shame and
dishonour that magnify themselves against me.

²⁷ Let them shout for joy, and be glad,
that favour my righteous cause:
yea, let them say continually,
'Let the Lord be magnified,
which hath pleasure in the prosperity
of his servant.'

²⁸ And my tongue shall speak of thy righteousness
and of thy praise all the day long.

36

To the chief musician, a psalm of David the servant of the Lord.

The transgression of the wicked
saith within my heart, that there is
no fear of God before his eyes.

² For he flattereth himself in his own eyes,
    until his iniquity be found to be hateful.
³ The words of his mouth are iniquity and deceit:
    he hath left off to be wise, and to do good.
⁴ He deviseth mischief upon his bed;
    he setteth himself in a way that is not good;
        he abhorreth not evil.
⁵ Thy mercy, O Lord, is in the heavens;
    and thy faithfulness reacheth
        unto the clouds.
⁶ Thy righteousness is like the great mountains;
    thy judgments are a great deep:
        O Lord, thou preservest man and beast.
⁷ How excellent is thy lovingkindness, O God!
    Therefore the children of men put their trust
        under the shadow of thy wings.
⁸ They shall be abundantly satisfied with the fatness
    of thy house; and thou shalt make them drink
        of the river of thy pleasures.
⁹ For with thee is the fountain of life:
    in thy light shall we see light.
¹⁰ O continue thy lovingkindness
    unto them that know thee;
        and thy righteousness
        to the upright in heart.
¹¹ Let not the foot of pride come against me,
    and let not the hand of the wicked remove me.
¹² There are the workers of iniquity fallen:

they are cast down,
>> and shall not be able to rise.

37 A psalm of David.

Fret not thyself because of evildoers,
>> neither be thou envious
>>> against the workers of iniquity.
2 For they shall soon be cut down like the grass,
>> and wither as the green herb.
3 Trust in the Lord, and do good;
>> so shalt thou dwell in the land,
>>> and verily thou shalt be fed.
4 Delight thyself also in the Lord;
>> and he shall give thee the desires of thine heart.
5 Commit thy way unto the Lord;
>> trust also in him; and he shall bring it to pass.
6 And he shall bring forth thy righteousness
>> as the light, and thy judgment as the noonday.
7 Rest in the Lord, and wait patiently for him:
>> fret not thyself because of him who prospereth
>>> in his way, because of the man who bringeth
>>> wicked devices to pass.
8 Cease from anger, and forsake wrath:
>> fret not thyself in any wise to do evil.
9 For evildoers shall be cut off:
>> but those that wait upon the Lord,
>>> they shall inherit the earth.

¹⁰ For yet a little while, and the wicked shall not be:
　　yea, thou shalt diligently consider his place,
　　　　and it shall not be.
¹¹ But the meek shall inherit the earth;
　　and shall delight themselves
　　　　in the abundance of peace.
¹² The wicked plotteth against the just,
　　and gnasheth upon him with his teeth.
¹³ The Lord shall laugh at him:
　　for he seeth that his day is coming.
¹⁴ The wicked have drawn out the sword,
　　and have bent their bow,
　　　　to cast down the poor and needy,
　　and to slay such as be of upright conversation.
¹⁵ Their sword shall enter into their own heart,
　　and their bows shall be broken.
¹⁶ A little that a righteous man hath
　　is better than the riches of many wicked.
¹⁷ For the arms of the wicked shall be broken;
　　but the Lord upholdeth the righteous.
¹⁸ The Lord knoweth the days of the upright:
　　and their inheritance shall be for ever.
¹⁹ They shall not be ashamed in the evil time:
　　and in the days of famine they shall be satisfied.
²⁰ But the wicked shall perish, and the enemies
　　of the Lord shall be as the fat of lambs;
　　　　they shall consume;
　　into smoke shall they consume away.

²¹ The wicked borroweth, and payeth not again;
  but the righteous sheweth mercy, and giveth.
²² For such as be blessed of him
    shall inherit the earth;
        and they that be cursed of him
    shall be cut off.
²³ The steps of a good man are ordered by the Lord,
  and he delighteth in his way.
²⁴ Though he fall, he shall not be utterly cast down;
  for the Lord upholdeth him with his hand.
²⁵ I have been young, and now am old;
    yet have I not seen the righteous forsaken,
        nor his seed begging bread.
²⁶ He is ever merciful, and lendeth;
  and his seed is blessed.
²⁷ Depart from evil, and do good;
  and dwell for evermore.
²⁸ For the Lord loveth judgment,
    and forsaketh not his saints;
        they are preserved for ever;
    but the seed of the wicked shall be cut off.
²⁹ The righteous shall inherit the land,
  and dwell therein for ever.
³⁰ The mouth of the righteous speaketh wisdom,
  and his tongue talketh of judgment.
³¹ The law of his God is in his heart;
  none of his steps shall slide.
³² The wicked watcheth the righteous,
  and seeketh to slay him.

³³ The Lord will not leave him in his hand,
nor condemn him when he is judged.
³⁴ Wait on the Lord, and keep his way,
and he shall exalt thee to inherit the land:
when the wicked are cut off,
thou shalt see it.
³⁵ I have seen the wicked in great power,
and spreading himself like a green bay tree.
³⁶ Yet he passed away, and, lo, he was not:
yea, I sought him, but he could not be found.
³⁷ Mark the perfect man, and behold the upright;
for the end of that man is peace.
³⁸ But the transgressors shall be destroyed together:
the end of the wicked shall be cut off.
³⁹ But the salvation of the righteous is of the Lord:
he is their strength in the time of trouble.
⁴⁰ And the Lord shall help them, and deliver them:
he shall deliver them from the wicked, and save
them, because they trust in him.

38

A psalm of David, to bring to remembrance.

O Lord, rebuke me not in thy wrath:
neither chasten me in thy hot displeasure.
² For thine arrows stick fast in me,
and thy hand presseth me sore.
³ There is no soundness in my flesh
because of thine anger;

neither is there any rest in my bones
because of my sin.
⁴ For mine iniquities are gone over mine head:
as an heavy burden
they are too heavy for me.
⁵ My wounds stink and are corrupt
because of my foolishness.
⁶ I am troubled; I am bowed down greatly;
I go mourning all the day long.
⁷ For my loins are filled with a loathsome disease:
and there is no soundness in my flesh.
⁸ I am feeble and sore broken:
I have roared by reason of the disquietness
of my heart.
⁹ Lord, all my desire is before thee;
and my groaning is not hid from thee.
¹⁰ My heart panteth, my strength faileth me:
as for the light of mine eyes,
it also is gone from me.
¹¹ My lovers and my friends stand aloof from my sore;
and my kinsmen stand afar off.
¹² They also that seek after my life lay snares for me:
and they that seek my hurt
speak mischievous things,
and imagine deceits all the day long.
¹³ But I, as a deaf man, heard not;
and I was as a dumb man that openeth not
his mouth.

¹⁴ Thus I was as a man that heareth not,
   and in whose mouth are no reproofs.
¹⁵ For in thee, O Lord, do I hope:
   thou wilt hear, O Lord my God.
¹⁶ For I said, 'Hear me, lest otherwise they should
   rejoice over me: when my foot slippeth,
   they magnify themselves against me.'
¹⁷ For I am ready to halt,
   and my sorrow is continually before me.
¹⁸ For I will declare mine iniquity;
   I will be sorry for my sin.
¹⁹ But mine enemies are lively, and they are strong:
   and they that hate me wrongfully
      are multiplied.
²⁰ They also that render evil for good
   are mine adversaries;
      because I follow the thing that good is.
²¹ Forsake me not, O Lord:
   O my God, be not far from me.
²² Make haste to help me, O Lord my salvation.

39   To the chief musician, even to Jeduthun,
      a psalm of David.

I said, I will take heed to my ways,
   that I sin not with my tongue:
      I will keep my mouth with a bridle,
      while the wicked is before me.

²I was dumb with silence, I held my peace,
   even from good;
      and my sorrow was stirred.
³My heart was hot within me, while I was musing
   the fire burned: then spake I with my tongue,
⁴'Lord, make me to know mine end,
   and the measure of my days, what it is;
      that I may know how frail I am.
⁵Behold, thou hast made my days
   as an handbreadth;
      and mine age is as nothing before thee:
      verily every man at his best state
         is altogether vanity. Selah.
⁶Surely every man walketh in a vain shew:
   surely they are disquieted in vain:
      he heapeth up riches,
      and knoweth not who shall gather them.
⁷And now, Lord, what wait I for?
   My hope is in thee.
⁸Deliver me from all my transgressions:
   make me not the reproach of the foolish.
⁹I was dumb, I opened not my mouth;
   because thou didst it.
¹⁰Remove thy stroke away from me:
   I am consumed by the blow of thine hand.
¹¹When thou with rebukes
   dost correct man for iniquity,
      thou makest his beauty to consume away
      like a moth: surely every man is vanity, Selah.

¹² Hear my prayer, O Lord, and give ear unto my cry;
  hold not thy peace at my tears;
    for I am a stranger with thee, and a sojourner,
  as all my fathers were.
¹³ O spare me, that I may recover strength,
  before I go hence, and be no more.'

40 To the chief musician, a psalm of David.

I waited patiently for the Lord;
  and he inclined unto me, and heard my cry.
² He brought me up also out of an horrible pit,
  out of the miry clay,
    and set my feet upon a rock,
  and established my goings.
³ And he hath put a new song in my mouth,
  even praise unto our God:
    many shall see it, and fear,
  and shall trust in the Lord.
⁴ Blessed is that man that maketh the Lord his trust,
  and respecteth not the proud,
    nor such as turn aside to lies.
⁵ Many, O Lord my God, are thy wonderful works
  which thou hast done,
    and thy thoughts which are to us-ward:
  they cannot be reckoned up in order unto thee:
    if I would declare and speak of them,
  they are more than can be numbered.

⁶ Sacrifice and offering thou didst not desire;
   mine ears hast thou opened:
      burnt offering and sin offering
   hast thou not required.
⁷ Then said I, 'Lo, I come:
   in the volume of the book
      it is written of me,
⁸ I delight to do thy will, O my God:
   yea, thy law is within my heart.'
⁹ I have preached righteousness in the great
   congregation: lo, I have not refrained my lips,
      O Lord, thou knowest.
¹⁰ I have not hid thy righteousness within my heart;
   I have declared thy faithfulness
      and thy salvation;
   I have not concealed thy lovingkindness
      and thy truth from the
   great congregation.
¹¹ Withhold not thou thy tender mercies from me,
   O Lord: let thy lovingkindness
      and thy truth continually preserve me.
¹² For innumerable evils have compassed me about:
   mine iniquities have taken hold upon me,
      so that I am not able to look up;
   they are more than the hairs of mine head;
      therefore my heart faileth me.
¹³ Be pleased, O Lord, to deliver me:
   O Lord, make haste to help me.

¹⁴ Let them be ashamed and confounded together
that seek after my soul to destroy it;
let them be driven backward
and put to shame that wish me evil.
¹⁵ Let them be desolate for a reward of their shame
that say unto me, 'Aha, aha.'
¹⁶ Let all those that seek thee rejoice
and be glad in thee:
let such as love thy salvation say continually,
'The Lord be magnified.'
¹⁷ But I am poor and needy;
yet the Lord thinketh upon me:
thou art my help and my deliverer;
make no tarrying, O my God.

41 To the chief musician, a psalm of David.

Blessed is he that considereth the poor:
the Lord will deliver him in time of trouble.
² The Lord will preserve him, and keep him alive;
and he shall be blessed upon the earth;
and thou wilt not deliver him
unto the will of his enemies.
³ The Lord will strengthen him
upon the bed of languishing:
thou wilt make all his bed in his sickness.
⁴ I said, 'Lord, be merciful unto me:
heal my soul; for I have sinned against thee.'

⁵Mine enemies speak evil of me,
  'When shall he die, and his name perish?'
⁶And if he come to see me, he speaketh vanity:
  his heart gathereth iniquity to itself;
    when he goeth abroad, he telleth it.
⁷All that hate me whisper together against me:
  against me do they devise my hurt.
⁸An evil disease, say they, cleaveth fast unto him:
  and now that he lieth he shall rise up no more.
⁹Yea, mine own familiar friend, in whom I trusted,
  which did eat of my bread,
    hath lifted up his heel against me.
¹⁰But thou, O Lord, be merciful unto me,
  and raise me up, that I may requite them.
¹¹By this I know that thou favourest me,
  because mine enemy doth not triumph over me.
¹²And as for me, thou upholdest me in mine integrity,
  and settest me before thy face for ever.
¹³Blessed be the Lord God of Israel from everlasting,
  and to everlasting. Amen, and Amen.

42 To the chief musician, Maschil, for the sons
   of Korah.

As the hart panteth after the water brooks,
  so panteth my soul after thee, O God.
²My soul thirsteth for God, for the living God:
  when shall I come and appear before God?

³ My tears have been my meat day and night,
  while they continually say unto me,
    'Where is thy God?'
⁴ When I remember these things,
  I pour out my soul in me;
      for I had gone with the multitude,
  I went with them to the house of God,
    with the voice of joy and praise,
  with a multitude that kept holyday.
⁵ Why art thou cast down, O my soul?
  And why art thou disquieted in me?
      Hope thou in God;
  for I shall yet praise him for the help of his
    countenance.
⁶ O my God, my soul is cast down within me;
  therefore will I remember thee
    from the land of Jordan,
  and of the Hermonites, from the hill Mizar.
⁷ Deep calleth unto deep at the noise
  of thy waterspouts: all thy waves and thy billows
    are gone over me.
⁸ Yet the Lord will command his lovingkindness
  in the daytime,
      and in the night his song shall be with me,
  and my prayer unto the God of my life.
⁹ I will say unto God my rock,
  'Why hast thou forgotten me?
    Why go I mourning because of

the oppression of the enemy?'
¹⁰As with a sword in my bones,
    mine enemies reproach me;
        while they say daily unto me,
    'Where is thy God?'
¹¹Why art thou cast down, O my soul?
    And why art thou disquieted within me?
        Hope thou in God;
    for I shall yet praise him, who is the health
        of my countenance, and my God.

43 Judge me, O God, and plead my cause
    against an ungodly nation:
        O deliver me from the deceitful
    and unjust man.
² For thou art the God of my strength:
    why dost thou cast me off?
        Why go I mourning because of
    the oppression of the enemy?
³ O send out thy light and thy truth:
    let them lead me;
        let them bring me unto thy holy hill,
    and to thy tabernacles.
⁴ Then will I go unto the altar of God,
    unto God my exceeding joy:
        yea, upon the harp will I praise thee,
    O God my God.

⁵ Why art thou cast down, O my soul?
    And why art thou disquieted within me?
        Hope in God; for I shall yet praise him,
    who is the health of my countenance,
        and my God.

44 To the chief musician, for the sons of Korah, Maschil.

We have heard with our ears, O God,
    our fathers have told us, what work thou didst
        in their days, in the times of old.
² How thou didst drive out the heathen with thy
    hand, and plantedst them;
        how thou didst afflict the people,
    and cast them out.
³ For they got not the land in possession
    by their own sword,
        neither did their own arm save them;
    but thy right hand, and thine arm,
        and the light of thy countenance,
    because thou hadst a favour unto them.
⁴ Thou art my King, O God:
    command deliverances for Jacob.
⁵ Through thee will we push down our enemies:
    through thy name will we tread them under
        that rise up against us.
⁶ For I will not trust in my bow,

neither shall my sword save me.
⁷ But thou hast saved us from our enemies,
    and hast put them to shame that hated us.
⁸ In God we boast all the day long,
    and praise thy name for ever. Selah.
⁹ But thou hast cast off, and put us to shame;
    and goest not forth with our armies.
¹⁰ Thou makest us to turn back from the enemy:
    and they which hate us spoil for themselves.
¹¹ Thou hast given us like sheep appointed for meat;
    and hast scattered us among the heathen.
¹² Thou sellest thy people for nought,
    and dost not increase thy wealth by their price.
¹³ Thou makest us a reproach to our neighbours,
    a scorn and a derision to them
        that are round about us.
¹⁴ Thou makest us a byword among the heathen,
    a shaking of the head among the people.
¹⁵ My confusion is continually before me,
    and the shame of my face hath covered me,
¹⁶ for the voice of him that reproacheth
    and blasphemeth;
        by reason of the enemy and avenger.
¹⁷ All this is come upon us;
    yet have we not forgotten thee,
        neither have we dealt falsely in thy covenant.
¹⁸ Our heart is not turned back,
    neither have our steps declined from thy way;

[19] though thou hast sore broken us
in the place of dragons,
and covered us with the shadow of death.
[20] If we have forgotten the name of our God,
or stretched out our hands to a strange god,
[21] shall not God search this out?
For he knoweth the secrets of the heart.
[22] Yea, for thy sake are we killed all the day long;
we are counted as sheep for the slaughter.
[23] Awake, why sleepest thou, O Lord?
Arise, cast us not off for ever.
[24] Wherefore hidest thou thy face,
and forgettest our affliction and our oppression?
[25] For our soul is bowed down to the dust:
our belly cleaveth unto the earth.
[26] Arise for our help,
and redeem us for thy mercies' sake.

45 To the chief musician upon Shoshannim,
for the sons of Korah, Maschil, a song of loves.

My heart is inditing a good matter:
I speak of the things which I have made
touching the king:
my tongue is the pen of a ready writer.
[2] Thou art fairer than the children of men:
grace is poured into thy lips;

therefore God hath blessed thee for ever.
³ Gird thy sword upon thy thigh, O most mighty,
    with thy glory and thy majesty.
⁴ And in thy majesty ride prosperously
    because of truth and meekness
        and righteousness;
    and thy right hand shall teach thee
        terrible things.
⁵ Thine arrows are sharp in the heart
    of the king's enemies;
        whereby the people fall under thee.
⁶ Thy throne, O God, is for ever and ever:
    the sceptre of thy kingdom is a right sceptre.
⁷ Thou lovest righteousness, and hatest wickedness;
    therefore God, thy God, hath anointed thee
        with the oil of gladness above thy fellows.
⁸ All thy garments smell of myrrh, and aloes,
    and cassia, out of the ivory palaces,
        whereby they have made thee glad.
⁹ Kings' daughters were among
    thy honourable women:
        upon thy right hand did stand the queen
    in gold of Ophir.
¹⁰ Hearken, O daughter, and consider, and incline
    thine ear; forget also thine own people,
        and thy father's house;
¹¹ so shall the king greatly desire thy beauty;
    for he is thy Lord; and worship thou him.

¹²And the daughter of Tyre shall be there with a gift;
even the rich among the people
shall intreat thy favour.
¹³The king's daughter is all glorious within;
her clothing is of wrought gold.
¹⁴She shall be brought unto the king
in raiment of needlework:
the virgins her companions that follow her
shall be brought unto thee.
¹⁵With gladness and rejoicing shall they be brought:
they shall enter into the king's palace.
¹⁶Instead of thy fathers shall be thy children,
whom thou mayest make princes
in all the earth.
¹⁷I will make thy name to be remembered
in all generations; therefore shall the people
praise thee for ever and ever.

46 To the chief musician for the sons of Korah,
a song upon Alamoth.

God is our refuge and strength,
a very present help in trouble.
²Therefore will not we fear,
though the earth be removed,
and though the mountains be carried
into the midst of the sea;
³though the waters thereof roar and be troubled,

though the mountains shake
with the swelling thereof. Selah.
⁴ There is a river, the streams whereof
shall make glad the city of God, the holy place
of the tabernacles of the most High.
⁵ God is in the midst of her; she shall not be moved:
God shall help her, and that right early.
⁶ The heathen raged, the kingdoms were moved:
he uttered his voice, the earth melted.
⁷ The Lord of hosts is with us;
the God of Jacob is our refuge. Selah.
⁸ Come, behold the works of the Lord,
what desolations he hath made in the earth.
⁹ He maketh wars to cease unto the end of the earth;
he breaketh the bow,
and cutteth the spear in sunder;
he burneth the chariot in the fire.
¹⁰ Be still, and know that I am God:
I will be exalted among the heathen,
I will be exalted in the earth.
¹¹ The Lord of hosts is with us;
the God of Jacob is our refuge. Selah.

47 To the chief musician, a psalm for
the sons of Korah.

O clap your hands, all ye people;
shout unto God with the voice of triumph.

² For the Lord most high is terrible;
    he is a great King over all the earth.
³ He shall subdue the people under us,
    and the nations under our feet.
⁴ He shall choose our inheritance for us,
    the excellency of Jacob whom he loved. Selah.
⁵ God is gone up with a shout,
    the Lord with the sound of a trumpet.
⁶ Sing praises to God, sing praises:
    sing praises unto our King, sing praises.
⁷ For God is the King of all the earth:
    sing ye praises with understanding.
⁸ God reigneth over the heathen:
    God sitteth upon the throne of his holiness.
⁹ The princes of the people are gathered together,
    even the people of the God of Abraham:
        for the shields of the earth belong unto God:
    he is greatly exalted.

48 A song and psalm for the sons of Korah.

Great is the Lord, and greatly to be praised
    in the city of our God,
        in the mountain of his holiness.
² Beautiful for situation, the joy of the whole earth,
    is mount Zion, on the sides of the north,
        the city of the great King.

³ God is known in her palaces for a refuge.
⁴ For, lo, the kings were assembled,
    they passed by together.
⁵ They saw it, and so they marvelled;
    they were troubled, and hasted away.
⁶ Fear took hold upon them there, and pain,
    as of a woman in travail.
⁷ Thou breakest the ships of Tarshish
    with an east wind.
⁸ As we have heard, so have we seen
    in the city of the Lord of hosts,
        in the city of our God:
    God will establish it for ever. Selah.
⁹ We have thought of thy lovingkindness, O God,
    in the midst of thy temple.
¹⁰ According to thy name, O God,
    so is thy praise unto the ends of the earth:
        thy right hand is full of righteousness.
¹¹ Let mount Zion rejoice,
    let the daughters of Judah be glad,
        because of thy judgments.
¹² Walk about Zion, and go round about her:
    tell the towers thereof.
¹³ Mark ye well her bulwarks, consider her palaces;
    that ye may tell it to the
        generation following.
¹⁴ For this God is our God for ever and ever:
    he will be our guide even unto death.

49

To the chief musician, a psalm for the sons of Korah.

Hear this, all ye people;
>give ear, all ye inhabitants of the world:
² both low and high, rich and poor,
>together.
³ My mouth shall speak of wisdom;
>and the meditation of my heart
>>shall be of understanding.
⁴ I will incline mine ear to a parable:
>I will open my dark saying upon the harp.
⁵ Wherefore should I fear in the days of evil,
>when the iniquity of my heels
>>shall compass me about?
⁶ They that trust in their wealth,
>and boast themselves in the multitude
>>of their riches;
⁷ none of them can by any means
>redeem his brother,
>>nor give to God a ransom for him
⁸ (for the redemption of their soul is precious,
>and it ceaseth for ever);
⁹ that he should still live for ever,
>and not see corruption.
¹⁰ For he seeth that wise men die,
>likewise the fool and the brutish person perish,
>>and leave their wealth to others.

¹¹ Their inward thought is,
    that their houses shall continue for ever,
        and their dwelling places to all generations;
    they call their lands after their own names.
¹² Nevertheless man being in honour abideth not:
    he is like the beasts that perish.
¹³ This their way is their folly:
    yet their posterity approve their sayings. Selah.
¹⁴ Like sheep they are laid in the grave;
    death shall feed on them;
        and the upright shall have dominion over
        them in the morning;
        and their beauty shall consume in the grave
        from their dwelling.
¹⁵ But God will redeem my soul from the power
    of the grave;
        for he shall receive me. Selah.
¹⁶ Be not thou afraid when one is made rich,
    when the glory of his house is increased;
¹⁷ for when he dieth he shall carry nothing away:
    his glory shall not descend after him.
¹⁸ Though while he lived he blessed his soul:
    and men will praise thee,
        when thou doest well to thyself.
¹⁹ He shall go to the generation of his fathers;
    they shall never see light.
²⁰ Man that is in honour, and understandeth not,
    is like the beasts that perish.

50

A psalm of Asaph.

The mighty God, even the Lord, hath spoken,
  and called the earth from the rising of the sun
    unto the going down thereof.
2 Out of Zion, the perfection of beauty,
  God hath shined.
3 Our God shall come, and shall not keep silence:
  a fire shall devour before him,
    and it shall be very tempestuous
  round about him.
4 He shall call to the heavens from above,
  and to the earth,
    that he may judge his people.
5 Gather my saints together unto me;
  those that have made a covenant with me
    by sacrifice.
6 And the heavens shall declare his righteousness;
  for God is judge himself. Selah.
7 Hear, O my people, and I will speak;
  O Israel, and I will testify against thee:
    I am God, even thy God.
8 I will not reprove thee for thy sacrifices
  or thy burnt offerings,
    to have been continually before me.
9 I will take no bullock out of thy house,
  nor he goats out of thy folds.
10 For every beast of the forest is mine,
  and the cattle upon a thousand hills.

¹¹ I know all the fowls of the mountains:
> and the wild beasts of the field are mine.

¹² If I were hungry, I would not tell thee;
> for the world is mine, and the fulness thereof.

¹³ Will I eat the flesh of bulls,
> or drink the blood of goats?

¹⁴ Offer unto God thanksgiving;
> and pay thy vows unto the most High;

¹⁵ and call upon me in the day of trouble:
> I will deliver thee,
>> and thou shalt glorify me.

¹⁶ But unto the wicked God saith,
> 'What hast thou to do to declare my statutes,
>> or that thou shouldest take my covenant in
> thy mouth?

¹⁷ Seeing thou hatest instruction,
> and castest my words behind thee.

¹⁸ When thou sawest a thief,
> then thou consentedst with him,
> and hast been partaker with adulterers.

¹⁹ Thou givest thy mouth to evil,
> and thy tongue frameth deceit.

²⁰ Thou sittest and speakest against thy brother;
> thou slanderest thine own mother's son.

²¹ These things hast thu done, and I kept silence;
> thou thoughtest that I was altogether
>> such an one as thyself; but I will reprove thee,
> and set them in order before thine eyes.

²² Now consider this, ye that forget God,
  lest I tear you in pieces,
    and there be none to deliver.
²³ Whoso offereth praise glorifieth me;
  and to him that ordereth his conversation aright
    will I shew the salvation of God.'

51 To the chief musician, a psalm of David,
  when Nathan the prophet came unto him,
  after he had gone in to Bath-sheba.

Have mercy upon me, O God,
  according to thy lovingkindness:
    according unto the multitude
  of thy tender mercies blot out my transgressions.
² Wash me throughly from mine iniquity,
  and cleanse me from my sin.
³ For I acknowledge my transgressions:
  and my sin is ever before me.
⁴ Against thee, thee only, have I sinned,
  and done this evil in thy sight:
    that thou mightest be justified
  when thou speakest,
    and be clear when thou judgest.
⁵ Behold, I was shapen in iniquity;
  and in sin did my mother conceive me.
⁶ Behold, thou desirest truth in the inward parts;
  and in the hidden part thou shalt make me

to know wisdom.

⁷ Purge me with hyssop, and I shall be clean:
    wash me, and I shall be whiter than snow.

⁸ Make me to hear joy and gladness;
    that the bones which thou hast broken
      may rejoice.

⁹ Hide thy face from my sins,
    and blot out all mine iniquities.

¹⁰ Create in me a clean heart, O God;
    and renew a right spirit within me.

¹¹ Cast me not away from thy presence;
    and take not thy holy spirit from me.

¹² Restore unto me the joy of thy salvation;
    and uphold me with thy free spirit.

¹³ Then will I teach transgressors thy ways;
    and sinners shall be converted unto thee.

¹⁴ Deliver me from bloodguiltiness, O God,
    thou God of my salvation;
      and my tongue shall sing aloud
    of thy righteousness.

¹⁵ O Lord, open thou my lips;
    and my mouth shall shew forth thy praise.

¹⁶ For thou desirest not sacrifice;
    else would I give it:
      thou delightest not in burnt offering.

¹⁷ The sacrifices of God are a broken spirit:
    a broken and a contrite heart, O God,
      thou wilt not despise.

¹⁸ Do good in thy good pleasure unto Zion:
>   build thou the walls of Jerusalem.
¹⁹ Then shalt thou be pleased with the sacrifices
>   of righteousness,
>   with burnt offering and whole burnt offering:
>   then shall they offer bullocks upon thine altar.

52 To the chief musician, Maschil, a psalm of David,
>   when Doeg the Edomite came and told Saul,
>   and said unto him,

'David is come to the house of Ahimelech.'
Why boastest thou thyself in mischief,
>   O mighty man?
>   The goodness of God
>   endureth continually.
² Thy tongue deviseth mischiefs;
>   like a sharp razor, working deceitfully.
³ Thou lovest evil more than good;
>   and lying rather than to speak
>   righteousness. Selah.
⁴ Thou lovest all devouring words,
>   O thou deceitful tongue.
⁵ God shall likewise destroy thee for ever,
>   he shall take thee away, and pluck thee out of
>   thy dwelling place,
>   and root thee out of the land
>   of the living. Selah.

6 The righteous also shall see, and fear,
  and shall laugh at him:
7 Lo, this is the man that made not God his strength;
  but trusted in the abundance of his riches,
    and strengthened himself
  in his wickedness.'
8 But I am like a green olive tree in the house of God:
  I trust in the mercy of God for ever and ever.
9 I will praise thee for ever, because thou hast done it:
  and I will wait on thy name;
    for it is good before thy saints.

53 To the chief musician upon Mahalath, Maschil,
     a psalm of David.

The fool hath said in his heart, 'There is no God.'
  Corrupt are they, and have done abominable
    iniquity: there is none that doeth good.
2 God looked down from heaven upon
    the children of men,
      to see if there were any that did understand,
    that did seek God.
3 Every one of them is gone back;
  they are altogether become filthy;
    there is none that doeth good, no, not one.
4 Have the workers of iniquity no knowledge?
  Who eat up my people as they eat bread:
    they have not called upon God.

⁵ There were they in great fear, where no fear was;
  for God hath scattered the bones of him
    that encampeth against thee:
  thou hast put them to shame,
    because God hath despised them.
⁶ Oh that the salvation of Israel
  were come out of Zion!
    When God bringeth back the captivity
  of his people,
    Jacob shall rejoice, and Israel shall be glad.

54 To the chief musician on Neginoth, Maschil,
   a psalm of David, when the Ziphims
   came and said to Saul,
   'Doth not David hide himself with us?'

Save me, O God, by thy name,
  and judge me by thy strength.
² Hear my prayer, O God;
  give ear to the words of my mouth.
³ For strangers are risen up against me,
  and oppressors seek after my soul:
    they have not set God before them. Selah.
⁴ Behold, God is mine helper:
  the Lord is with them that uphold my soul.
⁵ He shall reward evil unto mine enemies,
  cut them off in thy truth.
⁶ I will freely sacrifice unto thee:

I will praise thy name, O Lord; for it is good.
⁷ For he hath delivered me out of all trouble;
    and mine eye hath seen his desire
        upon mine enemies.

55

To the chief musician on Neginoth, Maschil, a psalm of David.

Give ear to my prayer, O God;
    and hide not thyself from my supplication.
² Attend unto me, and hear me:
    I mourn in my complaint, and make a noise;
³ because of the voice of the enemy,
    because of the oppression of the wicked;
        for they cast iniquity upon me,
    and in wrath they hate me.
⁴ My heart is sore pained within me;
    and the terrors of death are fallen upon me.
⁵ Fearfulness and trembling are come upon me,
    and horror hath overwhelmed me.
⁶ And I said, 'Oh that I had wings like a dove!
    For then would I fly away, and be at rest.
⁷ Lo, then would I wander far off,
    and remain in the wilderness. Selah.
⁸ I would hasten my escape from the windy storm
    and tempest.'
⁹ Destroy, O Lord, and divide their tongues;
    for I have seen violence and strife in the city.

¹⁰ Day and night they go about it
    upon the walls thereof: mischief also and sorrow
        are in the midst of it.
¹¹ Wickedness is in the midst thereof:
    deceit and guile depart not from her streets.
¹² For it was not an enemy that reproached me;
    then I could have borne it:
        neither was it he that hated me that did
    magnify himself against me;
        then I would have hid myself from him.
¹³ But it was thou, a man mine equal,
    my guide, and mine acquaintance.
¹⁴ We took sweet counsel together, and walked
    unto the house of God in company.
¹⁵ Let death seize upon them,
    and let them go down quick into hell;
        for wickedness is in their dwellings,
    and among them.
¹⁶ As for me, I will call upon God;
    and the Lord shall save me.
¹⁷ Evening, and morning, and at noon,
    will I pray, and cry aloud;
        and he shall hear my voice.
¹⁸ He hath delivered my soul in peace
    from the battle that was against me;
        for there were many with me.
¹⁹ God shall hear, and afflict them,
    even he that abideth of old. Selah.

Because they have no changes,
therefore they fear not God.
²⁰ He hath put forth his hands against such as
be at peace with him:
he hath broken his covenant.
²¹ The words of his mouth were smoother than butter,
but war was in his heart:
his words were softer than oil,
yet were they drawn swords.
²² Cast thy burden upon the Lord,
and he shall sustain thee: he shall
never suffer the righteous to be moved.
²³ But thou, O God, shalt bring them down
into the pit of destruction:
bloody and deceitful men shall not live out
half their days; but I will trust in thee.

56 To the chief musician upon Jonath-elem-rechokim,
Michtam of David, when the Philistines
took him in Gath.

Be merciful unto me, O God;
for man would swallow me up;
he fighting daily oppresseth me.
² Mine enemies would daily swallow me up;
for they be many that fight against me,
O thou most High.

³ What time I am afraid, I will trust in thee.
⁴ In God I will praise his word,
     in God I have put my trust;
          I will not fear what flesh can do unto me.
⁵ Every day they wrest my words:
     all their thoughts are against me for evil.
⁶ They gather themselves together,
     they hide themselves, they mark my steps,
          when they wait for my soul.
⁷ Shall they escape by iniquity?
     In thine anger cast down the people, O God.
⁸ Thou tellest my wanderings:
     put thou my tears into thy bottle:
          are they not in thy book?
⁹ When I cry unto thee,
          then shall mine enemies turn back:
     this I know; for God is for me.
¹⁰ In God will I praise his word:
     in the Lord will I praise his word.
¹¹ In God have I put my trust:
     I will not be afraid
          what man can do unto me.
¹² Thy vows are upon me, O God:
     I will render praises unto thee.
¹³ For thou hast delivered my soul from death:
     wilt not thou deliver my feet from falling,
          that I may walk before God
     in the light of the living?

57 To the chief musician, Al-taschith, Michtam
of David, when he fled from Saul in the cave.

Be merciful unto me, O God,
be merciful unto me; for my soul trusteth in thee:
yea, in the shadow of thy wings
will I make my refuge,
until these calamities be overpast.
² I will cry unto God most high;
unto God that performeth all things for me.
³ He shall send from heaven,
and save me from the reproach of him
that would swallow me up. Selah.
God shall send forth his mercy and his truth.
⁴ My soul is among lions;
and I lie even among them that are set on fire,
even the sons of men,
whose teeth are spears and arrows,
and their tongue a sharp sword.
⁵ Be thou exalted, O God, above the heavens;
let thy glory be above all the earth.
⁶ They have prepared a net for my steps;
my soul is bowed down;
they have digged a pit before me,
into the midst whereof they are fallen
themselves. Selah.
⁷ My heart is fixed, O God, my heart is fixed;
I will sing and give praise.

⁸Awake up, my glory;
    awake, psaltery and harp:
        I myself will awake early.
⁹ I will praise thee, O Lord, among the people:
    I will sing unto thee among the nations.
¹⁰ For thy mercy is great unto the heavens,
    and thy truth unto the clouds.
¹¹ Be thou exalted, O God, above the heavens:
    let thy glory be above all the earth.

58

To the chief musician, Al-taschith, Michtam of David.

Do ye indeed speak righteousness, O congregation?
    Do ye judge uprightly, O ye sons of men?
² Yea, in heart ye work wickedness;
    ye weigh the violence of your hands
        in the earth.
³ The wicked are estranged from the womb:
    they go astray as soon as they be born,
        speaking lies.
⁴ Their poison is like the poison of a serpent:
    they are like the deaf adder that stoppeth her ear,
⁵ which will not hearken to the voice of charmers,
    charming never so wisely.
⁶ Break their teeth, O God, in their mouth:
    break out the great teeth of the young lions,
        O Lord.

⁷ Let them melt away as waters
> which run continually:
>> when he bendeth his bow to shoot his arrows,
>> let them be as cut in pieces.
⁸ As a snail which melteth,
> let every one of them pass away:
>> like the untimely birth of a woman,
>> that they may not see the sun.
⁹ Before your pots can feel the thorns,
> he shall take them away as with a whirlwind,
>> both living, and in his wrath.
¹⁰ The righteous shall rejoice
> when he seeth the vengeance:
>> he shall wash his feet in the blood
>> of the wicked.
¹¹ So that a man shall say,
> 'Verily there is a reward for the righteous:
>> verily he is a God that judgeth in the earth.'

59

To the chief musician, Al-taschith, Michtam
of David; when Saul sent, and they watched
the house to kill him.

Deliver me from mine enemies, O my God:
> defend me from them that rise up against me.
² Deliver me from the workers of iniquity,
> and save me from bloody men.

³ For, lo, they lie in wait for my soul:
the mighty are gathered against me;
not for my transgression,
nor for my sin, O Lord.
⁴ They run and prepare themselves without my fault:
awake to help me, and behold.
⁵ Thou therefore, O Lord God of hosts,
the God of Israel, awake to visit all the heathen:
be not merciful
to any wicked transgressors. Selah.
⁶ They return at evening:
they make a noise like a dog,
and go round about the city.
⁷ Behold, they belch out with their mouth;
swords are in their lips;
for 'Who,' say they, 'doth hear?'
⁸ But thou, O Lord, shalt laugh at them;
thou shalt have all the heathen in derision.
⁹ Because of his strength will I wait upon thee;
for God is my defence.
¹⁰ The God of my mercy shall prevent me:
God shall let me see my desire
upon mine enemies.
¹¹ Slay them not, lest my people forget:
scatter them by thy power;
and bring them down, O Lord our shield.
¹² For the sin of their mouth
and the words of their lips

let them even be taken in their pride;
and for cursing and lying which they speak.

¹³ Consume them in wrath, consume them,
that they may not be;
and let them know that God ruleth in Jacob
unto the ends of the earth. Selah.

¹⁴ And at evening let them return;
and let them make a noise like a dog,
and go round about the city.

¹⁵ Let them wander up and down for meat,
and grudge if they be not satisfied.

¹⁶ But I will sing of thy power;
yea, I will sing aloud of thy mercy
in the morning;
for thou hast been my defence and refuge in the
day of my trouble.

¹⁷ Unto thee, O my strength, will I sing;
for God is my defence, and the God of my mercy.

60

To the chief musician upon Shushan-eduth,
Michtam of David, to teach; when he strove
with Aram-naharaim and with Aram-zobah,
when Joab returned, and smote of Edom
in the valley of salt twelve thousand.

O God, thou hast cast us off, thou hast scattered us,
thou hast been displeased;
O turn thyself to us again.

² Thou hast made the earth to tremble;
>> thou hast broken it:
>>> heal the breaches thereof, for it shaketh.
³ Thou hast shewed thy people hard things:
>> thou hast made us to drink
>>> the wine of astonishment.
⁴ Thou hast given a banner to them that fear thee,
>> that it may be displayed
>>> because of the truth. Selah.
⁵ That thy beloved may be delivered;
>> save with thy right hand, and hear me.
⁶ God hath spoken in his holiness:
>> 'I will rejoice, I will divide Shechem,
>>> and mete out the valley of Succoth.
⁷ Gilead is mine, and Manasseh is mine;
>> Ephraim also is the strength of mine head;
>>> Judah is my lawgiver;
⁸ Moab is my washpot;
>> over Edom will I cast out my shoe;
>>> Philistia, triumph thou because of me.'
⁹ Who will bring me into the strong city?
>> Who will lead me into Edom?
¹⁰ Wilt not thou, O God, which hadst cast us off?
>> And thou, O God, which didst not go out
>>> with our armies?
¹¹ Give us help from trouble;
>> for vain is the help of man.
¹² Through God we shall do valiantly;
>> for he it is that shall tread down our enemies.

61 To the chief musician upon Neginah,
      a psalm of David.

Hear my cry, O God; attend unto my prayer.
² From the end of the earth will I cry unto thee,
      when my heart is overwhelmed:
            lead me to the rock that is higher than I.
³ For thou hast been a shelter for me,
      and a strong tower from the enemy.
⁴ I will abide in thy tabernacle for ever:
      I will trust in the covert of thy wings. Selah.
⁵ For thou, O God, hast heard my vows:
      thou hast given me the heritage
            of those that fear thy name.
⁶ Thou wilt prolong the king's life;
      and his years as many generations.
⁷ He shall abide before God for ever:
      O prepare mercy and truth,
            which may preserve him.
⁸ So will I sing praise unto thy name for ever,
      that I may daily perform my vows.

62 To the chief musician, to Jeduthun,
      a psalm of David.

Truly my soul waiteth upon God:
      from him cometh my salvation.
² He only is my rock and my salvation;
      he is my defence; I shall not be greatly moved.

³ How long will ye imagine mischief against a man?
   Ye shall be slain all of you:
      as a bowing wall shall ye be,
   and as a tottering fence.
⁴ They only consult to cast him down
   from his excellency: they delight in lies:
      they bless with their mouth,
   but they curse inwardly. Selah.
⁵ My soul, wait thou only upon God;
   for my expectation is from him.
⁶ He only is my rock and my salvation;
   he is my defence; I shall not be moved.
⁷ In God is my salvation and my glory:
   the rock of my strength,
      and my refuge, is in God.
⁸ Trust in him at all times;
   ye people, pour out your heart before him:
      God is a refuge for us. Selah.
⁹ Surely men of low degree are vanity,
   and men of high degree are a lie:
      to be laid in the balance,
   they are altogether lighter than vanity.
¹⁰ Trust not in oppression,
   and become not vain in robbery:
      if riches increase, set not your heart upon them.
¹¹ God hath spoken once; twice have I heard this;
      that power belongeth unto God.
¹² Also unto thee, O Lord, belongeth mercy:

for thou renderest to every man
according to his work.

63 A psalm of David, when he was in the wilderness
of Judah.

O God, thou art my God; early will I seek thee:
my soul thirsteth for thee,
my flesh longeth for thee
in a dry and thirsty land,
where no water is,
2 to see thy power and thy glory,
so as I have seen thee in the sanctuary.
3 Because thy lovingkindness is better than life,
my lips shall praise thee.
4 Thus will I bless thee while I live:
I will lift up my hands in thy name.
5 My soul shall be satisfied as with marrow
and fatness; and my mouth shall praise thee
with joyful lips:
6 when I remember thee upon my bed,
and meditate on thee in the night watches.
7 Because thou hast been my help,
therefore in the shadow of thy wings
will I rejoice.
8 My soul followeth hard after thee:
thy right hand upholdeth me.

⁹ But those that seek my soul, to destroy it,
    shall go into the lower parts of the earth.
¹⁰ They shall fall by the sword:
    they shall be a portion for foxes.
¹¹ But the king shall rejoice in God;
    every one that sweareth by him shall glory:
        but the mouth of them that speak lies
        shall be stopped.

64

To the chief musician, a psalm of David.

Hear my voice, O God, in my prayer:
    preserve my life from fear of the enemy.
² Hide me from the secret counsel of the wicked;
    from the insurrection
        of the workers of iniquity,
³ who whet their tongue like a sword,
    and bend their bows to shoot their arrows,
        even bitter words,
⁴ that they may shoot in secret at the perfect:
    suddenly do they shoot at him, and fear not.
⁵ They encourage themselves in an evil matter:
    they commune of laying snares privily;
        they say, 'Who shall see them?'
⁶ They search out iniquities;
    they accomplish a diligent search:
        both the inward thought of every one of them,

and the heart, is deep.
⁷ But God shall shoot at them with an arrow;
    suddenly shall they be wounded.
⁸ So they shall make their own tongue
    to fall upon themselves:
        all that see them shall flee away.
⁹ And all men shall fear, and shall declare
    the work of God;
        for they shall wisely consider of his doing.
¹⁰ The righteous shall be glad in the Lord,
    and shall trust in him;
        and all the upright in heart shall glory.

65

To the chief musician, a psalm and song of David.

Praise waiteth for thee, O God, in Sion:
    and unto thee shall the vow be performed.
² O thou that hearest prayer,
    unto thee shall all flesh come.
³ Iniquities prevail against me:
    as for our transgressions,
        thou shalt purge them away.
⁴ Blessed is the man whom thou choosest,
    and causest to approach unto thee,
        that he may dwell in thy courts:
    we shall be satisfied with the goodness
        of thy house, even of thy holy temple.

⁵ By terrible things in righteousness
   wilt thou answer us,
       O God of our salvation;
   who art the confidence of all the ends
       of the earth,
   and of them that are afar off upon the sea;
⁶ Which by his strength setteth fast the mountains;
   being girded with power;
⁷ Which stilleth the noise of the seas,
   the noise of their waves,
       and the tumult of the people.
⁸ They also that dwell in the uttermost parts
   are afraid at thy tokens:
       thou makest the outgoings of the morning
   and evening to rejoice.
⁹ Thou visitest the earth, and waterest it:
   thou greatly enrichest it with the river of God,
       which is full of water:
   thou preparest them corn,
       when thou hast so provided for it.
¹⁰ Thou waterest the ridges thereof abundantly:
   thou settlest the furrows thereof:
       thou makest it soft with showers:
   thou blessest the springing thereof.
¹¹ Thou crownest the year with thy goodness;
   and thy paths drop fatness.
¹² They drop upon the pastures of the wilderness:
   and the little hills rejoice on every side.

¹³ The pastures are clothed with flocks;
    the valleys also are covered over with corn;
        they shout for joy, they also sing.

66 To the chief musician, a song or psalm.

Make a joyful noise unto God, all ye lands:
² sing forth the honour of his name:
    make his praise glorious.
³ Say unto God,
    'How terrible art thou in thy works!
        Through the greatness of thy power
    shall thine enemies submit
        themselves unto thee.
⁴ All the earth shall worship thee,
    and shall sing unto thee;
        they shall sing to thy name.' Selah.
⁵ Come and see the works of God:
    he is terrible in his doing toward
        the children of men.
⁶ He turned the sea into dry land:
    they went through the flood on foot:
        there did we rejoice in him.
⁷ He ruleth by his power for ever;
    his eyes behold the nations: let not
        the rebellious exalt themselves. Selah.
⁸ O bless our God, ye people,
    and make the voice of his praise to be heard,

⁹ Which holdeth our soul in life,
    and suffereth not our feet to be moved.
¹⁰ For thou, O God, hast proved us:
    thou hast tried us, as silver is tried.
¹¹ Thou broughtest us into the net;
    thou laidst affliction upon our loins.
¹² Thou hast caused men to ride over our heads;
    we went through fire and through water:
        but thou broughtest us out
    into a wealthy place.
¹³ I will go into thy house with burnt offerings:
    I will pay thee my vows,
¹⁴ which my lips have uttered, and my mouth hath
    spoken, when I was in trouble.
¹⁵ I will offer unto thee burnt sacrifices of fatlings,
    with the incense of rams;
        I will offer bullocks with goats. Selah.
¹⁶ Come and hear, all ye that fear God,
    and I will declare what he hath done
        for my soul.
¹⁷ I cried unto him with my mouth,
    and he was extolled with my tongue.
¹⁸ If I regard iniquity in my heart,
    the Lord will not hear me:
¹⁹ but verily God hath heard me;
    he hath attended to the voice of my prayer.
²⁰ Blessed be God, which hath not turned away
    my prayer, nor his mercy from me.

67 To the chief musician on Neginoth, a psalm or song.

God be merciful unto us, and bless us;
  and cause his face to shine upon us; Selah.
² That thy way may be known upon earth,
  thy saving health among all nations.
³ Let the people praise thee, O God;
  let all the people praise thee.
⁴ O let the nations be glad and sing for joy:
  for thou shalt judge the people righteously,
    and govern the nations upon earth. Selah.
⁵ Let the people praise thee, O God;
  let all the people praise thee.
⁶ Then shall the earth yield her increase;
  and God, even our own God, shall bless us.
⁷ God shall bless us; and all the ends of the earth
  shall fear him.

68 To the chief musician, a psalm or song of David.

Let God arise, let his enemies be scattered:
  let them also that hate him flee before him.
² As smoke is driven away, so drive them away:
  as wax melteth before the fire,
    so let the wicked perish
  at the presence of God.
³ But let the righteous be glad;
  let them rejoice before God;
    yea, let them exceedingly rejoice.

⁴ Sing unto God, sing praises to his name:
    extol him that rideth upon the heavens
        by his name JAH, and rejoice before him.
⁵ A father of the fatherless, and a judge
    of the widows, is God in his holy habitation.
⁶ God setteth the solitary in families:
    he bringeth out those which are bound
        with chains:
    but the rebellious dwell in a dry land.
⁷ O God, when thou wentest forth before thy people,
    when thou didst march through
        the wilderness; Selah;
⁸ the earth shook, the heavens also dropped
    at the presence of God;
        even Sinai itself was moved at the presence
    of God, the God of Israel.
⁹ Thou, O God, didst send a plentiful rain,
    whereby thou didst confirm thine inheritance,
        when it was weary.
¹⁰ Thy congregation hath dwelt therein:
    thou, O God, hast prepared of thy goodness
        for the poor.
¹¹ The Lord gave the word:
    great was the company of those that published it.
¹² Kings of armies did flee apace:
    and she that tarried at home divided the spoil.
¹³ Though ye have lien among the pots, yet shall ye be
    as the wings of a dove covered with silver,
        and her feathers with yellow gold.

¹⁴ When the Almighty scattered kings in it,
    it was white as snow in Salmon.
¹⁵ The hill of God is as the hill of Bashan;
    an high hill as the hill of Bashan.
¹⁶ Why leap ye, ye high hills?
    This is the hill which God desireth to dwell in;
        yea, the Lord will dwell in it for ever.
¹⁷ The chariots of God are twenty thousand,
    even thousands of angels:
        the Lord is among them, as in Sinai,
    in the holy place.
¹⁸ Thou hast ascended on high,
    thou hast led captivity captive;
        thou hast received gifts for men;
    yea, for the rebellious also,
        that the Lord God might dwell among them.
¹⁹ Blessed be the Lord, who daily loadeth us
    with benefits,
        even the God of our salvation. Selah.
²⁰ He that is our God is the God of salvation;
    and unto God the Lord belong the issues
        from death.
²¹ But God shall wound the head of his enemies,
    and the hairy scalp of such an one as goeth
        on still in his trespasses.
²² The Lord said,
    'I will bring again from Bashan,
        I will bring my people again
    from the depths of the sea,

²³ that thy foot may be dipped
in the blood of thine enemies,
and the tongue of thy dogs in the same.'
²⁴ They have seen thy goings, O God;
even the goings of my God, my King,
in the sanctuary.
²⁵ The singers went before,
the players on instruments followed after;
among them were the damsels
playing with timbrels.
²⁶ Bless ye God in the congregations,
even the Lord, from the fountain of Israel.
²⁷ There is little Benjamin with their ruler,
the princes of Judah and their council,
the princes of Zebulun,
and the princes of Naphtali.
²⁸ Thy God hath commanded thy strength:
strengthen, O God, that which thou hast
wrought for us.
²⁹ Because of thy temple at Jerusalem shall kings
bring presents unto thee.
³⁰ Rebuke the company of spearmen,
the multitude of the bulls,
with the calves of the people, till every one
submit himself with pieces of silver:
scatter thou the people that delight in war.
³¹ Princes shall come out of Egypt;
Ethiopia shall soon stretch out her hands
unto God.

³² Sing unto God, ye kingdoms of the earth;
O sing praises unto the Lord; Selah;
³³ to him that rideth upon the heavens of heavens,
which were of old;
lo, he doth send out his voice, and that a
mighty voice.
³⁴ Ascribe ye strength unto God:
his excellency is over Israel,
and his strength is in the clouds.
³⁵ O God, thou art terrible out of thy holy places:
the God of Israel is he that giveth strength
and power unto his people.
Blessed be God.

69 To the chief musician upon Shoshannim,
a psalm of David.

Save me, O God; for the waters are come in
unto my soul.
² I sink in deep mire, where there is no standing:
I am come into deep waters,
where the floods overflow me.
³ I am weary of my crying: my throat is dried:
mine eyes fail while I wait for my God.
⁴ They that hate me without a cause are
more than the hairs of mine head:
they that would destroy me,
being mine enemies wrongfully, are mighty:
then I restored that which I took not away.

⁵ O God, thou knowest my foolishness;
   and my sins are not hid from thee.
⁶ Let not them that wait on thee, O Lord God of hosts,
   be ashamed for my sake: let not those that seek thee
      be confounded for my sake, O God of Israel.
⁷ Because for thy sake I have borne reproach;
   shame hath covered my face.
⁸ I am become a stranger unto my brethren,
   and an alien unto my mother's children.
⁹ For the zeal of thine house hath eaten me up;
   and the reproaches of them that reproached thee
      are fallen upon me.
¹⁰ When I wept, and chastened my soul with fasting,
   that was to my reproach.
¹¹ I made sackcloth also my garment;
   and I became a proverb to them.
¹² They that sit in the gate speak against me;
   and I was the song of the drunkards.
¹³ But as for me, my prayer is unto thee, O Lord,
   in an acceptable time: O God,
      in the multitude of thy mercy hear me,
   in the truth of thy salvation.
¹⁴ Deliver me out of the mire, and let me not sink:
   let me be delivered from them that hate me,
      and out of the deep waters.
¹⁵ Let not the waterflood overflow me,
   neither let the deep swallow me up,
      and let not the pit shut her mouth upon me.

¹⁶ Hear me, O Lord; for thy loving-kindness is good:
    turn unto me according to the multitude
    of thy tender mercies.
¹⁷ And hide not thy face from thy servant;
    for I am in trouble: hear me speedily.
¹⁸ Draw nigh unto my soul, and redeem it:
    deliver me because of mine enemies.
¹⁹ Thou hast known my reproach,
    and my shame, and my dishonour:
        mine adversaries are all before thee.
²⁰ Reproach hath broken my heart;
    and I am full of heaviness;
        and I looked for some to take pity,
    but there was none;
        and for comforters, but I found none.
²¹ They gave me also gall for my meat;
    and in my thirst they gave me vinegar to drink.
²² Let their table become a snare before them:
    and that which should have been for their welfare,
        let it become a trap.
²³ Let their eyes be darkened, that they see not;
    and make their loins continually to shake.
²⁴ Pour out thine indignation upon them,
    and let thy wrathful anger take hold of them.
²⁵ Let their habitation be desolate;
    and let none dwell in their tents.
²⁶ For they persecute him whom thou hast smitten;
    and they talk to the grief of those
        whom thou hast wounded.

²⁷Add iniquity unto their iniquity:
     and let them not come into thy righteousness.
²⁸Let them be blotted out of the book of the living,
     and not be written with the righteous.
²⁹But I am poor and sorrowful:
     let thy salvation, O God, set me up on high.
³⁰I will praise the name of God with a song,
     and will magnify him with thanksgiving.
³¹This also shall please the Lord better than an ox
     or bullock that hath horns and hoofs.
³²The humble shall see this, and be glad;
     and your heart shall live that seek God.
³³For the Lord heareth the poor,
     and despiseth not his prisoners.
³⁴Let the heaven and earth praise him,
     the seas, and every thing that moveth therein.
³⁵For God will save Zion, and will build
     the cities of Judah: that they may dwell there,
          and have it in possession.
³⁶The seed also of his servants shall inherit it:
     and they that love his name shall dwell therein.

70 To the chief musician, a psalm of David,
     to bring to remembrance.

Make haste, O God, to deliver me;
     make haste to help me, O Lord.

² Let them be ashamed and confounded
  that seek after my soul:
    let them be turned backward,
    and put to confusion, that desire my hurt.
³ Let them be turned back for a reward
  of their shame that say, 'Aha, aha.'
⁴ Let all those that seek thee rejoice
  and be glad in thee:
    and let such as love thy salvation
    say continually, 'Let God be magnified.'
⁵ But I am poor and needy:
  make haste unto me, O God:
    thou art my help and my deliverer;
    O Lord, make no tarrying.

71 In thee, O Lord, do I put my trust:
     let me never be put to confusion.
² Deliver me in thy righteousness,
  and cause me to escape:
    incline thine ear unto me, and save me.
³ Be thou my strong habitation,
  where-unto I may continually resort:
    thou hast given commandment to save me;
    for thou art my rock and my fortress.
⁴ Deliver me, O my God, out of the hand
  of the wicked, out of the hand of the unrighteous
    and cruel man.

⁵ For thou art my hope, O Lord God:
     thou art my trust from my youth.
⁶ By thee have I been holden up from the womb:
     thou art he that took me out
          of my mother's bowels:
     my praise shall be continually of thee.
⁷ I am as a wonder unto many;
     but thou art my strong refuge.
⁸ Let my mouth be filled with thy praise
     and with thy honour all the day.
⁹ Cast me not off in the time of old age;
     forsake me not when my strength faileth.
¹⁰ For mine enemies speak against me;
     and they that lay wait for my soul
          take counsel together,
¹¹ Saying, 'God hath forsaken him:
     persecute and take him;
          for there is none to deliver him.'
¹² O God, be not far from me:
     O my God, make haste for my help.
¹³ Let them be confounded and consumed
     that are adversaries to my soul;
          let them be covered with reproach
     and dishonour that seek my hurt.
¹⁴ But I will hope continually,
     and will yet praise thee more and more.
¹⁵ My mouth shall shew forth thy righteousness
     and thy salvation all the day;
          for I know not the numbers thereof.

¹⁶ I will go in the strength of the Lord God:
    I will make mention of thy righteousness,
        even of thine only.
¹⁷ O God, thou hast taught me from my youth;
    and hitherto have I declared thy wondrous works.
¹⁸ Now also when I am old and gray-headed,
    O God, forsake me not;
        until I have shewed thy strength
    unto this generation,
        and thy power to every one that is to come.
¹⁹ Thy righteousness also, O God,
    is very high, who hast done great things:
        O God, who is like unto thee!
²⁰ Thou, which hast shewed me great
    and sore troubles, shalt quicken me again,
        and shalt bring me up again from the depths
    of the earth.
²¹ Thou shalt increase my greatness,
    and comfort me on every side.
²² I will also praise thee with the psaltery,
    even thy truth, O my God:
        unto thee will I sing with the harp,
    O thou Holy One of Israel.
²³ My lips shall greatly rejoice when I sing unto thee;
    and my soul, which thou hast redeemed.
²⁴ My tongue also shall talk of thy righteousness
    all the day long: for they are confounded,
        for they are brought unto shame,
    that seek my hurt.

72

A psalm for Solomon.

Give the king thy judgments, O God,
   and thy righteousness unto the king's son.
² He shall judge thy people with righteousness,
   and thy poor with judgment.
³ The mountains shall bring peace to the people,
   and the little hills, by righteousness.
⁴ He shall judge the poor of the people,
   he shall save the children of the needy,
      and shall break in pieces the oppressor.
⁵ They shall fear thee as long as the sun
   and moon endure,
      throughout all generations.
⁶ He shall come down like rain upon the mown grass,
   as showers that water the earth.
⁷ In his days shall the righteous flourish;
   and abundance of peace
      so long as the moon endureth.
⁸ He shall have dominion also from sea to sea,
   and from the river unto the ends of the earth.
⁹ They that dwell in the wilderness shall bow
   before him;
      and his enemies shall lick the dust.
¹⁰ The kings of Tarshish and of the isles
   shall bring presents:
      the kings of Sheba and Seba
   shall offer gifts.

¹¹ Yea, all kings shall fall down before him:
   all nations shall serve him.
¹² For he shall deliver the needy when he crieth;
   the poor also, and him that hath no helper.
¹³ He shall spare the poor and needy,
   and shall save the souls of the needy.
¹⁴ He shall redeem their soul from deceit
   and violence: and precious
      shall their blood be in his sight.
¹⁵ And he shall live, and to him shall be given
   of the gold of Sheba:
      prayer also shall be made for him continually;
   and daily shall he be praised.
¹⁶ There shall be an handful of corn in the earth
   upon the top of the mountains;
      the fruit thereof shall shake like Lebanon:
   and they of the city shall flourish
      like grass of the earth.
¹⁷ His name shall endure for ever:
   his name shall be continued as long as the sun:
      and men shall be blessed in him:
   all nations shall call him blessed.
¹⁸ Blessed be the Lord God, the God of Israel,
   who only doeth wondrous things.
¹⁹ And blessed be his glorious name for ever:
   and let the whole earth be filled with his glory;
      Amen, and Amen.
²⁰ The prayers of David the son of Jesse are ended.

73 A psalm of Asaph.

Truly God is good to Israel,
  even to such as are of a clean heart.
2 But as for me, my feet were almost gone;
  my steps had well nigh slipped.
3 For I was envious at the foolish,
  when I saw the prosperity of the wicked.
4 For there are no bands in their death;
  but their strength is firm.
5 They are not in trouble as other men;
  neither are they plagued like other men.
6 Therefore pride compasseth them about as a chain;
  violence covereth them as a garment.
7 Their eyes stand out with fatness:
  they have more than heart could wish.
8 They are corrupt, and speak wickedly
  concerning oppression: they speak loftily.
9 They set their mouth against the heavens,
  and their tongue walketh through the earth.
10 Therefore his people return hither:
  and waters of a full cup are wrung out to them.
11 And they say, 'How doth God know?
  And is there knowledge in the most High?'
12 Behold, these are the ungodly,
  who prosper in the world; they increase in riches.
13 Verily I have cleansed my heart in vain,
  and washed my hands in innocency.

¹⁴ For all the day long have I been plagued,
and chastened every morning.
¹⁵ If I say, 'I will speak thus',
behold, I should offend against
the generation of thy children.
¹⁶ When I thought to know this,
it was too painful for me,
¹⁷ until I went into the sanctuary of God;
then understood I their end.
¹⁸ Surely thou didst set them in slippery places:
thou castedst them down into destruction.
¹⁹ How are they brought into desolation,
as in a moment!
They are utterly consumed with terrors.
²⁰ As a dream when one awaketh;
so, O Lord, when thou awakest,
thou shalt despise their image.
²¹ Thus my heart was grieved,
and I was pricked in my reins.
²² So foolish was I, and ignorant:
I was as a beast before thee.
²³ Nevertheless I am continually with thee:
thou hast holden me by my right hand.
²⁴ Thou shalt guide me with thy counsel,
and afterward receive me to glory.
²⁵ Whom have I in heaven but thee?
And there is none upon earth
that I desire beside thee.

²⁶ My flesh and my heart faileth;
  but God is the strength of my heart,
    and my portion for ever.
²⁷ For, lo, they that are far from thee shall perish:
  thou hast destroyed all them
    that go a whoring from thee.
²⁸ But it is good for me to draw near to God:
  I have put my trust in the Lord God,
    that I may declare all thy works.

74

Maschil of Asaph.

O God, why hast thou cast us off for ever?
  Why doth thine anger smoke
    against the sheep of thy pasture?
² Remember thy congregation,
  which thou hast purchased of old;
    the rod of thine inheritance,
  which thou hast redeemed;
    this mount Zion, wherein thou hast dwelt.
³ Lift up thy feet unto the perpetual desolations;
  even all that the enemy hath done
    wickedly in the sanctuary.
⁴ Thine enemies roar in the midst
  of thy congregations;
    they set up their ensigns for signs.
⁵ A man was famous according as he had lifted up
  axes upon the thick trees.

⁶ But now they break down the carved work thereof
at once with axes and hammers.
⁷ They have cast fire into thy sanctuary,
they have defiled by casting down
the dwelling place of thy name to the ground.
⁸ They said in their hearts,
'Let us destroy them together';
they have burned up all the synagogues
of God in the land.
⁹ We see not our signs: there is no more any prophet:
neither is there among us
any that knoweth how long.
¹⁰ O God, how long shall the adversary reproach?
Shall the enemy blaspheme thy name for ever?
¹¹ Why withdrawest thou thy hand, even thy right hand?
Pluck it out of thy bosom.
¹² For God is my King of old,
working salvation in the midst of the earth.
¹³ Thou didst divide the sea by thy strength:
thou brakest the heads of the dragons
in the waters.
¹⁴ Thou brakest the heads of leviathan in pieces,
and gavest him to be meat to the people
inhabiting the wilderness.
¹⁵ Thou didst cleave the fountain and the flood:
thou driedst up mighty rivers.
¹⁶ The day is thine, the night also is thine:
thou hast prepared the light and the sun.

¹⁷ Thou hast set all the borders of the earth:
   thou hast made summer and winter.
¹⁸ Remember this, that the enemy hath reproached,
    O Lord, and that the foolish people
       have blasphemed thy name.
¹⁹ O deliver not the soul of thy turtledove
    unto the multitude of the wicked:
       forget not the congregation
    of thy poor for ever.
²⁰ Have respect unto the covenant:
    for the dark places of the earth are full
       of the habitations of cruelty.
²¹ O let not the oppressed return ashamed:
    let the poor and needy praise thy name.
²² Arise, O God, plead thine own cause:
    remember how the foolish man
       reproacheth thee daily.
²³ Forget not the voice of thine enemies:
    the tumult of those that rise up against thee
       increaseth continually.

75

To the chief musician, Al-taschith,
   a psalm or song of Asaph.

Unto thee, O God, do we give thanks,
   unto thee do we give thanks;
      for that thy name is near
   thy wondrous works declare.

² When I shall receive the congregation
    I will judge uprightly.
³ The earth and all the inhabitants thereof are dissolved:
    I bear up the pillars of it. Selah.
⁴ I said unto the fools, 'Deal not foolishly,
    and to the wicked, 'Lift not up the horn;
⁵ lift not up your horn on high:
    speak not with a stiff neck.'
⁶ For promotion cometh neither from the east,
    nor from the west, nor from the south.
⁷ But God is the judge:
    he putteth down one, and setteth up another.
⁸ For in the hand of the Lord there is a cup,
    and the wine is red; it is full of mixture;
        and he poureth out of the same:
    but the dregs thereof, all the wicked
        of the earth shall wring them out,
    and drink them.
⁹ But I will declare for ever;
    I will sing praises to the God of Jacob.
¹⁰ All the horns of the wicked also will I cut off;
    but the horns of the righteous shall be exalted.

76 To the chief musician on Neginoth,
      a psalm or song of Asaph.

In Judah is God known: his name is great in Israel.

² In Salem also is his tabernacle,
and his dwelling place in Zion.
³ There brake he the arrows of the bow,
the shield and the sword, and the battle. Selah.
⁴ Thou art more glorious and excellent than
the mountains of prey.
⁵ The stouthearted are spoiled,
they have slept their sleep;
and none of the men of might
have found their hands.
⁶ At thy rebuke, O God of Jacob,
both the chariot and horse are cast
into a dead sleep.
⁷ Thou, even thou, art to be feared;
and who may stand in thy sight
when once thou art angry?
⁸ Thou didst cause judgment
to be heard from heaven;
the earth feared, and was still,
⁹ when God arose to judgment,
to save all the meek of the earth. Selah.
¹⁰ Surely the wrath of man shall praise thee:
the remainder of wrath shalt thou restrain.
¹¹ Vow, and pay unto the Lord your God:
let all that be round about him bring presents
unto him that ought to be feared.
¹² He shall cut off the spirit of princes:
he is terrible to the kings of the earth.

77

To the chief musician, to Jeduthun,
a psalm of Asaph.

I cried unto God with my voice,
even unto God with my voice;
and he gave ear unto me.
² In the day of my trouble I sought the Lord:
my sore ran in the night, and ceased not:
my soul refused to be comforted.
³ I remembered God,
and was troubled:
I complained, and my spirit
was overwhelmed. Selah.
⁴ Thou holdest mine eyes waking;
I am so troubled
that I cannot speak.
⁵ I have considered the days of old,
the years of ancient times.
⁶ I call to remembrance my song in the night:
I commune with mine own heart:
and my spirit made diligent search.
⁷ Will the Lord cast off for ever?
And will he be favourable no more?
⁸ Is his mercy clean gone for ever?
Doth his promise fail for evermore?
⁹ Hath God forgotten to be gracious?
Hath he in anger shut up
his tender mercies? Selah.

¹⁰And I said, 'This is my infirmity;
　　but I will remember the years of the right hand
　　　of the most High.'
¹¹I will remember the works of the Lord:
　　surely I will remember thy wonders of old.
¹²I will meditate also of all thy work,
　　and talk of thy doings.
¹³Thy way, O God, is in the sanctuary:
　　who is so great a God as our God?
¹⁴Thou art the God that doest wonders:
　　thou hast declared thy strength among
　　　the people.
¹⁵Thou hast with thine arm redeemed thy people,
　　the sons of Jacob and Joseph. Selah.
¹⁶The waters saw thee, O God,
　　the waters saw thee; they were afraid;
　　　the depths also were troubled.
¹⁷The clouds poured out water:
　　the skies sent out a sound:
　　　thine arrows also went abroad.
¹⁸The voice of thy thunder was in the heaven:
　　the lightnings lightened the world:
　　　the earth trembled and shook.
¹⁹Thy way is in the sea, and thy path
　　in the great waters,
　　　and thy footsteps are not known.
²⁰Thou leddest thy people like a flock
　　by the hand of Moses and Aaron.

78 Maschil of Asaph.

Give ear, O my people, to my law:
  incline your ears to the words of my mouth.
² I will open my mouth in a parable:
  I will utter dark sayings of old,
³ which we have heard and known,
  and our fathers have told us.
⁴ We will not hide them from their children,
  shewing to the generation to come the praises of
    the Lord, and his strength,
  and his wonderful works that he hath done.
⁵ For he established a testimony in Jacob,
  and appointed a law in Israel,
    which he commanded our fathers,
  that they should make them known
    to their children;
⁶ that the generation to come might know them,
  even the children which should be born;
    who should arise and declare them
  to their children;
⁷ that they might set their hope in God,
  and not forget the works of God,
    but keep his commandments;
⁸ and might not be as their fathers,
  a stubborn and rebellious generation;
    a generation that set not their heart aright,
  and whose spirit was not stedfast with God.

⁹ The children of Ephraim,
    being armed, and carrying bows,
        turned back in the day of battle.
¹⁰ They kept not the covenant of God,
    and refused to walk in his law;
¹¹ and forgat his works,
    and his wonders that he had shewed them.
¹² Marvellous things did he
    in the sight of their fathers,
        in the land of Egypt, in the field of Zoan.
¹³ He divided the sea,
    and caused them to pass through;
        and he made the waters to stand as an heap.
¹⁴ In the daytime also he led them with a cloud,
    and all the night with a light of fire.
¹⁵ He clave the rocks in the wilderness,
    and gave them drink as out of the great depths.
¹⁶ He brought streams also out of the rock,
    and caused waters to run down like rivers.
¹⁷ And they sinned yet more against him
    by provoking the most High in the wilderness.
¹⁸ And they tempted God in their heart
    by asking meat for their lust.
¹⁹ Yea, they spake against God; they said,
    'Can God furnish a table in the wilderness?'
²⁰ Behold, he smote the rock, that the waters gushed out,
    and the streams overflowed;
        can he give bread also?
    Can he provide flesh for his people?

²¹ Therefore the Lord heard this, and was wroth:
   so a fire was kindled against Jacob,
      and anger also came up against Israel;
²² because they believed not in God,
      and trusted not in his salvation,
²³ though he had commanded the clouds from above,
      and opened the doors of heaven,
²⁴ and had rained down manna upon them to eat,
      and had given them of the corn of heaven.
²⁵ Man did eat angels' food:
      he sent them meat to the full.
²⁶ He caused an east wind to blow in the heaven:
      and by his power he brought in the south wind.
²⁷ He rained flesh also upon them as dust,
      and feathered fowls like as the sand of the sea;
²⁸ and he let it fall in the midst of their camp,
      round about their habitations.
²⁹ So they did eat, and were well filled;
      for he gave them their own desire;
³⁰ they were not estranged from their lust.
      But while their meat was yet in their mouths,
³¹ the wrath of God came upon them,
      and slew the fattest of them,
         and smote down the chosen men of Israel.
³² For all this they sinned still,
      and believed not for his wondrous works.
³³ Therefore their days did he consume in vanity,
      and their years in trouble.

³⁴ When he slew them, then they sought him;
and they returned and enquired early after God.
³⁵ And they remembered that God was their rock,
and the high God their redeemer.
³⁶ Nevertheless they did flatter him with their mouth,
and they lied unto him with their tongues.
³⁷ For their heart was not right with him,
neither were they stedfast in his covenant.
³⁸ But he, being full of compassion, forgave
their iniquity, and destroyed them not:
yea, many a time turned he his anger away,
and did not stir up all his wrath.
³⁹ For he remembered that they were but flesh;
a wind that passeth away, and cometh not again.
⁴⁰ How oft did they provoke him in the wilderness,
and grieve him in the desert!
⁴¹ Yea, they turned back and tempted God,
and limited the Holy One of Israel.
⁴² They remembered not his hand,
nor the day when he delivered them
from the enemy.
⁴³ How he had wrought his signs in Egypt,
and his wonders in the field of Zoan;
⁴⁴ and had turned their rivers into blood;
and their floods, that they could not drink.
⁴⁵ He sent divers sorts of flies among them,
which devoured them;
and frogs, which destroyed them.

⁴⁶ He gave also their increase unto the caterpiller,
    and their labour unto the locust.
⁴⁷ He destroyed their vines with hail,
    and their sycomore trees with frost.
⁴⁸ He gave up their cattle also to the hail,
    and their flocks to hot thunderbolts.
⁴⁹ He cast upon them the fierceness of his anger,
    wrath, and indignation, and trouble,
        by sending evil angels among them.
⁵⁰ He made a way to his anger;
    he spared not their soul from death,
        but gave their life over to the pestilence;
⁵¹ and smote all the firstborn in Egypt;
    the chief of their strength in the tabernacles
        of Ham;
⁵² but made his own people to go forth like sheep,
    and guided them in the wilderness like a flock.
⁵³ And he led them on safely, so that they feared not;
    but the sea overwhelmed their enemies.
⁵⁴ And he brought them to the border
    of his sanctuary, even to this mountain,
        which his right hand had purchased.
⁵⁵ He cast out the heathen also before them,
    and divided them an inheritance by line,
        and made the tribes of Israel
    to dwell in their tents.
⁵⁶ Yet they tempted and provoked
    the most high God, and kept not his testimonies;

^{57} but turned back,
>> and dealt unfaithfully like their fathers:
>>> they were turned aside like a deceitful bow.
^{58} For they provoked him to anger
>> with their high places,
>>> and moved him to jealousy
>> with their graven images.
^{59} When God heard this, he was wroth,
>> and greatly abhorred Israel,
^{60} so that he forsook the tabernacle of Shiloh,
>> the tent which he placed among men;
^{61} and delivered his strength into captivity,
>> and his glory into the enemy's hand.
^{62} He gave his people over also unto the sword;
>> and was wroth with his inheritance.
^{63} The fire consumed their young men;
>> and their maidens were not given to marriage.
^{64} Their priests fell by the sword;
>> and their widows made no lamentation.
^{65} Then the Lord awaked as one out of sleep,
>> and like a mighty man that shouteth
>>> by reason of wine.
^{66} And he smote his enemies in the hinder parts:
>> he put them to a perpetual reproach.
^{67} Moreover he refused the tabernacle of Joseph,
>> and chose not the tribe of Ephraim,
^{68} but chose the tribe of Judah,
>> the mount Zion which he loved.

⁶⁹And he built his sanctuary like high palaces,
like the earth which he hath
established for ever.
⁷⁰He chose David also his servant,
and took him from the sheepfolds:
⁷¹from following the ewes great with young
he brought him to feed Jacob his people,
and Israel his inheritance.
⁷²So he fed them according to the integrity
of his heart; and guided them
by the skilfulness of his hands.

79

A psalm of Asaph.

O God, the heathen are come into thine inheritance;
thy holy temple have they defiled;
they have laid Jerusalem on heaps.
²The dead bodies of thy servants have they given
to be meat unto the fowls of the heaven,
the flesh of thy saints
unto the beasts of the earth.
³Their blood have they shed like water
round about Jerusalem;
and there was none to bury them.
⁴We are become a reproach to our neighbours,
a scorn and derision to them
that are round about us.

⁵ How long, Lord? Wilt thou be angry for ever?
    Shall thy jealousy burn like fire?
⁶ Pour out thy wrath upon the heathen
        that have not known thee, and upon the kingdoms
            that have not called upon thy name.
⁷ For they have devoured Jacob,
        and laid waste his dwelling place.
⁸ O remember not against us former iniquities:
        let thy tender mercies speedily prevent us,
            for we are brought very low.
⁹ Help us, O God of our salvation,
        for the glory of thy name:
            and deliver us, and purge away our sins,
        for thy name's sake.
¹⁰ Wherefore should the heathen say,
        'Where is their God?'
            Let him be known among the heathen
        in our sight by the revenging of the blood
            of thy servants which is shed.
¹¹ Let the sighing of the prisoner come before thee;
        according to the greatness of thy power
            preserve thou those that are appointed to die;
¹² and render unto our neighbours sevenfold
        into their bosom their reproach,
            wherewith they have reproached thee, O Lord.
¹³ So we thy people and sheep of thy pasture
        will give thee thanks for ever:
            we will shew forth thy praise to all generations.

80 To the chief musician upon Shoshannim-Eduth,
a psalm of Asaph.

Give ear, O Shepherd of Israel,
thou that leadest Joseph like a flock;
thou that dwellest between the cherubims,
shine forth.
² Before Ephraim and Benjamin and Manasseh
stir up thy strength, and come and save us.
³ Turn us again, O God, and cause thy face to shine;
and we shall be saved.
⁴ O Lord God of hosts, how long wilt thou be angry
against the prayer of thy people.
⁵ Thou feedest them with the bread of tears;
and givest them tears to drink in great measure.
⁶ Thou makest us a strife unto our neighbours;
and our enemies laugh among themselves.
⁷ Turn us again, O God of hosts,
and cause thy face to shine; and we shall be saved.
⁸ Thou hast brought a vine out of Egypt:
thou hast cast out the heathen, and planted it.
⁹ Thou preparedst room before it,
and didst cause it to take deep root,
and it filled the land.
¹⁰ The hills were covered with the shadow of it,
and the boughs thereof were
like the goodly cedars.
¹¹ She sent out her boughs unto the sea,
and her branches unto the river.

¹² Why hast thou then broken down her hedges,
so that all they which pass by the way
do pluck her?
¹³ The boar out of the wood doth waste it,
and the wild beast of the field doth devour it.
¹⁴ Return, we beseech thee, O God of hosts:
look down from heaven, and behold,
and visit this vine;
¹⁵ and the vineyard which thy right hand
hath planted, and the branch
that thou madest strong for thyself.
¹⁶ It is burned with fire, it is cut down:
they perish at the rebuke of thy countenance.
¹⁷ Let thy hand be upon the man of thy right hand,
upon the son of man
whom thou madest strong for thyself.
¹⁸ So will not we go back from thee:
quicken us, and we will call upon thy name.
¹⁹ Turn us again, O Lord God of hosts,
cause thy face to shine;
and we shall be saved.

81 To the chief musician upon Gittith,
a psalm of Asaph.

Sing aloud unto God our strength:
make a joyful noise unto the God of Jacob.
² Take a psalm, and bring hither the timbrel,
the pleasant harp with the psaltery.

³ Blow up the trumpet in the new moon,
  in the time appointed,
    on our solemn feast day.
⁴ For this was a statute for Israel,
  and a law of the God of Jacob.
⁵ This he ordained in Joseph for a testimony,
  when he went out through the land of Egypt,
    where I heard a language that I understood not.
⁶ I removed his shoulder from the burden:
  his hands were delivered from the pots.
⁷ Thou calledst in trouble, and I delivered thee;
  I answered thee in the secret place of thunder;
    I proved thee at the waters of Meribah. Selah.
⁸ Hear, O my people, and I will testify unto thee:
  O Israel, if thou wilt hearken unto me;
⁹ there shall no strange god be in thee;
  neither shalt thou worship any strange god.
¹⁰ I am the Lord thy God,
  which brought thee out of the land of Egypt:
    open thy mouth wide, and I will fill it.
¹¹ But my people would not hearken to my voice;
  and Israel would none of me.
¹² So I gave them up unto their own hearts' lust;
  and they walked in their own counsels.
¹³ Oh that my people had hearkened unto me,
  and Israel had walked in my ways!
¹⁴ I should soon have subdued their enemies,
  and turned my hand against their adversaries.

¹⁵ The haters of the Lord should have submitted
themselves unto him;
> but their time should have endured for ever.
¹⁶ He should have fed them also with
the finest of the wheat;
> and with honey out of the rock
should I have satisfied thee.

82

A psalm of Asaph.

God standeth in the congregation of the mighty;
he judgeth among the gods.
² How long will ye judge unjustly,
and accept the persons of the wicked? Selah.
³ Defend the poor and fatherless:
do justice to the afflicted and needy.
⁴ Deliver the poor and needy:
rid them out of the hand of the wicked.
⁵ They know not, neither will they understand;
they walk on in darkness:
> all the foundations of the earth
are out of course.
⁶ I have said, 'Ye are gods;
and all of you are children of the most High.
⁷ But ye shall die like men,
and fall like one of the princes.'
⁸ Arise, O God, judge the earth:
for thou shalt inherit all nations.

83

A song or psalm of Asaph.

Keep not thou silence, O God: hold not thy peace,
  and be not still, O God.
² For, lo, thine enemies make a tumult;
  and they that hate thee have lifted up the head.
³ They have taken crafty counsel against thy people,
  and consulted against thy hidden ones.
⁴ They have said, 'Come, and let us
  cut them off from being a nation;
    that the name of Israel may be
  no more in remembrance.'
⁵ For they have consulted together with one consent:
  they are confederate against thee:
⁶ the tabernacles of Edom, and the Ishmaelites;
  of Moab, and the Hagarenes;
⁷ Gebal, and Ammon, and Amalek;
  the Philistines with the inhabitants of Tyre;
⁸ Assur also is joined with them:
  they have holpen the children of Lot. Selah.
⁹ Do unto them as unto the Midianites;
  as to Sisera, as to Jabin, at the brook of Kison,
¹⁰ which perished at En-dor:
  they became as dung for the earth.
¹¹ Make their nobles like Oreb, and like Zeeb:
  yea, all their princes as Zebah, and as Zalmunna,
¹² who said, Let us take to ourselves
  the houses of God in possession.

¹³ O my God, make them like a wheel;
   as the stubble before the wind.
¹⁴ As the fire burneth a wood,
   and as the flame setteth the mountains on fire;
¹⁵ so persecute them with thy tempest,
   and make them afraid with thy storm.
¹⁶ Fill their faces with shame;
   that they may seek thy name, O Lord.
¹⁷ Let them be confounded and troubled for ever;
   yea, let them be put to shame, and perish,
¹⁸ that men may know that thou,
   whose name alone is Jehovah,
      art the most high over all the earth.

84

To the chief musician upon Gittith, a psalm for the sons of Korah.

How amiable are thy tabernacles, O Lord of hosts!
² My soul longeth, yea, even fainteth
   for the courts of the Lord:
      my heart and my flesh crieth out
   for the living God.
³ Yea, the sparrow hath found an house,
   and the swallow a nest for herself,
      where she may lay her young,
   even thine altars, O Lord of hosts,
      my King, and my God.
⁴ Blessed are they that dwell in thy house:

they will be still praising thee. Selah.
⁵ Blessed is the man whose strength is in thee:
    in whose heart are the ways of them.
⁶ Who passing through the valley of Baca
    make it a well;
        the rain also filleth the pools.
⁷ They go from strength to strength,
    every one of them in Zion appeareth before God.
⁸ O Lord God of hosts, hear my prayer:
    give ear, O God of Jacob. Selah.
⁹ Behold, O God our shield,
    and look upon the face of thine anointed.
¹⁰ For a day in thy courts is better than a thousand.
    I had rather be a doorkeeper
        in the house of my God,
    than to dwell in the tents of wickedness.
¹¹ For the Lord God is a sun and shield:
    the Lord will give grace and glory:
        no good thing will he withhold
    from them that walk uprightly.
¹² O Lord of hosts,
    blessed is the man that trusteth in thee.

85 To the chief musician, a psalm for the sons
    of Korah.

Lord, thou hast been favourable unto thy land:
    thou hast brought back the captivity of Jacob.

² Thou hast forgiven the iniquity of thy people,
    thou hast covered all their sin. Selah.
³ Thou hast taken away all thy wrath:
    thou hast turned thyself from the fierceness
      of thine anger.
⁴ Turn us, O God of our salvation,
    and cause thine anger toward us to cease.
⁵ Wilt thou be angry with us for ever?
    Wilt thou draw out thine anger
      to all generations?
⁶ Wilt thou not revive us again,
    that thy people may rejoice in thee?
⁷ Shew us thy mercy, O Lord,
    and grant us thy salvation.
⁸ I will hear what God the Lord will speak,
    for he will speak peace unto his people,
      and to his saints;
    but let them not turn again to folly.
⁹ Surely his salvation is nigh them that fear him;
    that glory may dwell in our land.
¹⁰ Mercy and truth are met together;
    righteousness and peace have kissed each other.
¹¹ Truth shall spring out of the earth;
    and righteousness shall look down
      from heaven.
¹² Yea, the Lord shall give that which is good;
    and our land shall yield her increase.
¹³ Righteousness shall go before him;
    and shall set us in the way of his steps.

86 A prayer of David.

Bow down thine ear, O Lord, hear me;
    for I am poor and needy.
² Preserve my soul; for I am holy:
    O thou my God, save thy servant
        that trusteth in thee.
³ Be merciful unto me, O Lord;
    for I cry unto thee daily.
⁴ Rejoice the soul of thy servant;
    for unto thee, O Lord, do I lift up my soul.
⁵ For thou, Lord, art good, and ready to forgive;
    and plenteous in mercy unto all them
        that call upon thee.
⁶ Give ear, O Lord, unto my prayer;
    and attend to the voice of my supplications.
⁷ In the day of my trouble I will call upon thee:
    for thou wilt answer me.
⁸ Among the gods there is none like unto thee,
    O Lord;
        neither are there any works
        like unto thy works.
⁹ All nations whom thou hast made
    shall come and worship before thee, O Lord;
        and shall glorify thy name.
¹⁰ For thou art great, and doest wondrous things:
    thou art God alone.
¹¹ Teach me thy way, O Lord; I will walk in thy truth:
    unite my heart to fear thy name.

¹²I will praise thee, O Lord my God, with all my heart:
    and I will glorify thy name for evermore.
¹³For great is thy mercy toward me: and thou hast
    delivered my soul from the lowest hell.
¹⁴O God, the proud are risen against me,
    and the assemblies of violent men
        have sought after my soul;
    and have not set thee before them.
¹⁵But thou, O Lord, art a God full of compassion,
    and gracious, longsuffering, and plenteous
        in mercy and truth.
¹⁶O turn unto me, and have mercy upon me;
    give thy strength unto thy servant,
        and save the son of thine handmaid.
¹⁷Shew me a token for good;
    that they which hate me may see it,
        and be ashamed, because thou, Lord,
    hast holpen me, and comforted me.

87 A psalm or song for the sons of Korah.

His foundation is in the holy mountains.
²The Lord loveth the gates of Zion
    more than all the dwellings of Jacob.
³Glorious things are spoken of thee,
    O city of God. Selah.
⁴I will make mention of Rahab and Babylon
    to them that know me: behold Philistia,

and Tyre, with Ethiopia;
this man was born there.
⁵And of Zion it shall be said,
'This and that man was born in her':
and the highest himself shall establish her.
⁶The Lord shall count,
when he writeth up the people,
that this man was born there. Selah.
⁷As well the singers as the players on instruments
shall be there: all my springs are in thee.

88 A song or psalm for the sons of Korah,
to the chief Musician upon Mahalath Leannoth,
Maschil of Heman the Ezrahite.

O Lord God of my salvation,
I have cried day and night before thee:
²let my prayer come before thee:
incline thine ear unto my cry,
³for my soul is full of troubles;
and my life draweth nigh unto the grave.
⁴I am counted with them that go down into the pit:
I am as a man that hath no strength;
⁵free among the dead, like the slain
that lie in the grave,
whom thou rememberest no more;
and they are cut off from thy hand.

⁶ Thou hast laid me in the lowest pit,
in darkness, in the deeps.
⁷ Thy wrath lieth hard upon me,
and thou hast afflicted me
with all thy waves. Selah.
⁸ Thou hast put a way mine acquaintance
far from me;
thou hast made me an abomination
unto them: I am shut up,
and I cannot come forth.
⁹ Mine eye mourneth by reason of affliction:
Lord, I have called daily upon thee,
I have stretched out my hands unto thee.
¹⁰ Wilt thou shew wonders to the dead?
Shall the dead arise and praise thee? Selah.
¹¹ Shall thy lovingkindness be declared in the grave?
Or thy faithfulness in destruction?
¹² Shall thy wonders be known in the dark?
And thy righteousness in the land
of forgetfulness?
¹³ But unto thee have I cried, O Lord;
and in the morning shall my prayer prevent thee.
¹⁴ Lord, why castest thou off my soul?
Why hidest thou thy face from me?
¹⁵ I am afflicted and ready to die from my youth up:
while I suffer thy terrors I am distracted.
¹⁶ Thy fierce wrath goeth over me;
thy terrors have cut me off.

¹⁷ They came round about me daily like water;
  they compassed me about together.
¹⁸ Lover and friend hast thou put far from me,
  and mine acquaintance into darkness.

89

Maschil of Ethan the Ezrahite.

I will sing of the mercies of the Lord for ever:
  with my mouth will I make known
  thy faithfulness to all generations.
² For I have said, 'Mercy shall be built up for ever:
  thy faithfulness shalt thou establish
    in the very heavens.'
³ I have made a covenant with my chosen,
  I have sworn unto David my servant,
⁴ 'Thy seed will I establish for ever,
  and build up thy throne to all generations.' Selah.
⁵ And the heavens shall praise thy wonders, O Lord:
  thy faithfulness also in the congregation
    of the saints.
⁶ For who in the heaven can be compared
  unto the Lord?
    Who among the sons of the mighty
    can be likened unto the Lord?
⁷ God is greatly to be feared in the assembly
  of the saints, and to be had in reverence
  of all them that are about him.

⁸ O Lord God of hosts, who is a strong Lord
   like unto thee?
      Or to thy faithfulness round about thee?
⁹ Thou rulest the raging of the sea:
   when the waves thereof arise, thou stillest them.
¹⁰ Thou hast broken Rahab in pieces,
   as one that is slain;
      thou hast scattered thine enemies
   with thy strong arm.
¹¹ The heavens are thine, the earth also is thine:
   as for the world and the fulness thereof,
      thou hast founded them.
¹² The north and the south thou hast created them:
   Tabor and Hermon shall rejoice in thy name.
¹³ Thou hast a mighty arm:
   strong is thy hand, and high is thy right hand.
¹⁴ Justice and judgment are the habitation
   of thy throne:
      mercy and truth shall go before thy face.
¹⁵ Blessed is the people that know the joyful sound:
   they shall walk, O Lord,
      in the light of thy countenance.
¹⁶ In thy name shall they rejoice all the day;
   and in thy righteousness shall they be exalted.
¹⁷ For thou art the glory of their strength;
   and in thy favour our horn shall be exalted.
¹⁸ For the Lord is our defence;
   and the Holy One of Israel is our king.

¹⁹ Then thou spakest in vision to thy holy one,
and saidst,

'I have laid help upon one that is mighty;
I have exalted one chosen out of the people.
²⁰ I have found David my servant;
with my holy oil have I anointed him,
²¹ with whom my hand shall be established:
mine arm also shall strengthen him.
²² The enemy shall not exact upon him;
nor the son of wickedness afflict him.
²³ And I will beat down his foes before his face,
and plague them that hate him.
²⁴ But my faithfulness and my mercy
shall be with him;

and in my name shall his horn be exalted.
²⁵ I will set his hand also in the sea,
and his right hand in the rivers.
²⁶ He shall cry unto me,

"Thou art my father, my God,
and the rock of my salvation."
²⁷ Also I will make him my firstborn,
higher than the kings of the earth.
²⁸ My mercy will I keep for him for evermore,
and my covenant shall stand fast with him.
²⁹ His seed also will I make to endure for ever,
and his throne as the days of heaven.
³⁰ If his children forsake my law,
and walk not in my judgments;

³¹ if they break my statutes,
and keep not my commandments;
³² then will I visit their transgression with the rod,
and their iniquity with stripes.
³³ Nevertheless my lovingkindness will I not
utterly take from him,
nor suffer my faithfulness to fail.
³⁴ My covenant will I not break,
nor alter the thing that is gone out of my lips.
³⁵ Once have I sworn by my holiness
that I will not lie unto David.
³⁶ His seed shall endure for ever,
and his throne as the sun before me.
³⁷ It shall be established for ever as the moon,
and as a faithful witness in heaven.' Selah.
³⁸ But thou hast cast off and abhorred,
thou hast been wroth with thine anointed.
³⁹ Thou hast made void the covenant of thy servant:
thou hast profaned his crown
by casting it to the ground.
⁴⁰ Thou hast broken down all his hedges;
thou hast brought his strong holds to ruin.
⁴¹ All that pass by the way spoil him:
he is a reproach to his neighbours.
⁴² Thou hast set up the right hand of his adversaries;
thou hast made all his enemies to rejoice.
⁴³ Thou hast also turned the edge of his sword,
and hast not made him to stand in the battle.

⁴⁴ Thou hast made his glory to cease,
and cast his throne down to the ground.
⁴⁵ The days of his youth hast thou shortened:
thou hast covered him with shame. Selah.
⁴⁶ How long, Lord?
Wilt thou hide thyself for ever?
Shall thy wrath burn like fire?
⁴⁷ Remember how short my time is:
wherefore hast thou made all men in vain?
⁴⁸ What man is he that liveth, and shall not see death?
Shall he deliver his soul from the hand
of the grave? Selah.
⁴⁹ Lord, where are thy former lovingkindnesses,
which thou swarest unto David in thy truth?
⁵⁰ Remember, Lord, the reproach of thy servants;
how I do bear in my bosom the reproach
of all the mighty people;
⁵¹ wherewith thine enemies have reproached, O Lord;
wherewith they have reproached the footsteps
of thine anointed.
⁵² Blessed be the Lord for evermore.
Amen, and Amen.

90

A prayer of Moses the man of God.

Lord, thou hast been our dwelling place
in all generations.

²Before the mountains were brought forth,
    or ever thou hadst formed the earth
        and the world,
    even from everlasting
        to everlasting, thou art God.
³Thou turnest man to destruction; and sayest,
    'Return, ye children of men.'
⁴For a thousand years in thy sight
    are but as yesterday when it is past,
        and as a watch in the night.
⁵Thou carriest them away as with a flood;
    they are as a sleep: in the morning they are like grass
        which groweth up.
⁶In the morning it flourisheth, and groweth up;
    in the evening it is cut down, and withereth.
⁷For we are consumed by thine anger,
    and by thy wrath are we troubled.
⁸Thou hast set our iniquities before thee,
    our secret sins in the light of thy countenance.
⁹For all our days are passed away in thy wrath:
    we spend our years as a tale that is told.
¹⁰The days of our years are three-score years and ten;
    and if by reason of strength
        they be fourscore years,
    yet is their strength labour and sorrow;
        for it is soon cut off, and we fly away.
¹¹Who knoweth the power of thine anger?
    Even according to thy fear, so is thy wrath.

¹² So teach us to number our days,
   that we may apply our hearts unto wisdom.
¹³ Return, O Lord, how long?
   And let it repent thee concerning thy servants.
¹⁴ O satisfy us early with thy mercy;
   that we may rejoice and be glad all our days.
¹⁵ Make us glad according to the days
   wherein thou hast afflicted us,
      and the years wherein we have seen evil.
¹⁶ Let thy work appear unto thy servants,
   and thy glory unto their children.
¹⁷ And let the beauty of the Lord our God be upon us;
   and establish thou the work of our hands upon us;
      yea, the work of our hands establish thou it.

91 He that dwelleth in the secret place of the most High
   shall abide under the shadow of the Almighty.
² I will say of the Lord,
   'He is my refuge and my fortress:
      my God; in him will I trust.'
³ Surely he shall deliver thee from the snare
   of the fowler,
      and from the noisome pestilence.
⁴ He shall cover thee with his feathers,
   and under his wings shalt thou trust:
      his truth shall be thy shield and buckler.
⁵ Thou shalt not be afraid for the terror by night;
   nor for the arrow that flieth by day;

⁶ nor for the pestilence that walketh in darkness;
    nor for the destruction that wasteth at noonday.
⁷ A thousand shall fall at thy side,
    and ten thousand at thy right hand;
        but it shall not come nigh thee.
⁸ Only with thine eyes shalt thou behold
    and see the reward of the wicked.
⁹ Because thou hast made the Lord,
    which is my refuge,
        even the most High, thy habitation;
¹⁰ there shall no evil befall thee,
    neither shall any plague come nigh thy dwelling.
¹¹ For he shall give his angels charge over thee,
    to keep thee in all thy ways.
¹² They shall bear thee up in their hands,
    lest thou dash thy foot against a stone.
¹³ Thou shalt tread upon the lion and adder:
    the young lion and the dragon
        shalt thou trample under feet.
¹⁴ Because he hath set his love upon me,
    therefore will I deliver him:
        I will set him on high,
    because he hath known my name.
¹⁵ He shall call upon me,
    and I will answer him;
        I will be with him in trouble;
    I will deliver him, and honour him.
¹⁶ With long life will I satisfy him,
    and shew him my salvation.

92

A psalm or song for the sabbath day.

It is a good thing to give thanks unto the Lord,
 and to sing praises unto thy name,
O most High,
² to shew forth thy lovingkindness in the morning,
 and thy faithfulness every night,
³ upon an instrument of ten strings,
 and upon the psaltery;
  upon the harp with a solemn sound.
⁴ For thou, Lord, hast made me glad
 through thy work:
  I will triumph in the works of thy hands.
⁵ O Lord, how great are thy works!
 And thy thoughts are very deep.
⁶ A brutish man knoweth not;
 neither doth a fool understand this.
⁷ When the wicked spring as the grass,
 and when all the workers of iniquity do flourish;
  it is that they shall be destroyed for ever;
⁸ but thou, Lord, art most high for evermore.
⁹ For, lo, thine enemies, O Lord,
 for, lo, thine enemies shall perish;
  all the workers of iniquity
 shall be scattered.
¹⁰ But my horn shalt thou exalt like the horn
 of an unicorn:
  I shall be anointed with fresh oil.

¹¹ Mine eye also shall see my desire on mine enemies,
and mine ears shall hear my desire
of the wicked that rise up against me.
¹² The righteous shall flourish like the palm tree:
he shall grow like a cedar in Lebanon.
¹³ Those that be planted in the house of the Lord
shall flourish in the courts of our God.
¹⁴ They shall still bring forth fruit in old age;
they shall be fat and flourishing;
¹⁵ to shew that the Lord is upright: he is my rock,
and there is no unrighteousness in him.

93 The Lord reigneth, he is clothed with majesty;
the Lord is clothed with strength,
wherewith he hath girded himself:
the world also is stablished,
that it cannot be moved.
² Thy throne is established of old:
thou art from everlasting.
³ The floods have lifted up, O Lord,
the floods have lifted up their voice;
the floods lift up their waves.
⁴ The Lord on high is mightier than the noise
of many waters,
yea, than the mighty waves of the sea.
⁵ Thy testimonies are very sure:
holiness becometh thine house, O Lord, for ever.

94 O Lord God, to whom vengeance belongeth;
    O God, to whom vengeance belongeth,
      shew thyself.
2 Lift up thyself, thou judge of the earth:
    render a reward to the proud.
3 Lord, how long shall the wicked,
    how long shall the wicked triumph?
4 How long shall they utter and speak hard things?
    And all the workers of iniquity boast themselves?
5 They break in pieces thy people, O Lord,
    and afflict thine heritage.
6 They slay the widow and the stranger,
    and murder the fatherless.
7 Yet they say, 'The Lord shall not see,
    neither shall the God of Jacob regard it.'
8 Understand, ye brutish among the people;
    and ye fools, when will ye be wise?
9 He that planted the ear, shall he not hear?
    He that formed the eye, shall he not see?
10 He that chastiseth the heathen,
    shall not he correct?
      He that teacheth man knowledge,
    shall not he know?
11 The Lord knoweth the thoughts of man,
    that they are vanity.
12 Blessed is the man whom thou chastenest,
    O Lord,
      and teachest him out of thy law;

¹³ that thou mayest give him rest
   from the days of adversity,
      until the pit be digged for the wicked.
¹⁴ For the Lord will not cast off his people,
   neither will he forsake his inheritance.
¹⁵ But judgment shall return unto righteousness;
   and all the upright in heart
      shall follow it.
¹⁶ Who will rise up for me against the evildoers?
   Or who will stand up for me
      against the workers of iniquity?
¹⁷ Unless the Lord had been my help,
   my soul had almost dwelt in silence.
¹⁸ When I said, 'My foot slippeth';
   thy mercy, O Lord, held me up.
¹⁹ In the multitude of my thoughts
   within me thy comforts delight my soul.
²⁰ Shall the throne of iniquity have fellowship
   with thee, which frameth mischief by a law?
²¹ They gather themselves together
   against the soul of the righteous,
      and condemn the innocent blood.
²² But the Lord is my defence;
   and my God is the rock of my refuge.
²³ And he shall bring upon them their own iniquity,
   and shall cut them off in their own wickedness;
      yea, the Lord our God
         shall cut them off.

95 O come, let us sing unto the Lord:
　　　let us make a joyful noise to the rock
　　　　of our salvation.
² Let us come before his presence with thanksgiving,
　　　and make a joyful noise
　　　　unto him with psalms.
³ For the Lord is a great God,
　　　and a great King above all gods.
⁴ In his hand are the deep places of the earth:
　　　the strength of the hills is his also.
⁵ The sea is his, and he made it;
　　　and his hands formed the dry land.
⁶ O come, let us worship and bow down:
　　　let us kneel before the Lord our maker.
⁷ For he is our God;
　　　and we are the people of his pasture,
　　　　and the sheep of his hand.
　　　To day if ye will hear his voice,
⁸ harden not your heart, as in the provocation,
　　　and as in the day of temptation in the wilderness;
⁹ when your fathers tempted me,
　　　proved me, and saw my work.
¹⁰ Forty years long was I grieved with this generation,
　　　and said,
　　　　'It is a people that do err in their heart,
　　　　and they have not known my ways,'
¹¹ unto whom I sware in my wrath that they should
　　　not enter into my rest.

96

O sing unto the Lord a new song:
   sing unto the Lord, all the earth.
² Sing unto the Lord, bless his name;
   shew forth his salvation from day to day.
³ Declare his glory among the heathen,
   his wonders among all people.
⁴ For the Lord is great, and greatly to be praised:
   he is to be feared above all gods.
⁵ For all the gods of the nations are idols;
   but the Lord made the heavens.
⁶ Honour and majesty are before him:
   strength and beauty are in his sanctuary.
⁷ Give unto the Lord, O ye kindreds of the people,
   give unto the Lord glory and strength.
⁸ Give unto the Lord the glory due unto his name:
   bring an offering, and come into his courts.
⁹ O worship the Lord in the beauty of holiness:
   fear before him, all the earth.
¹⁰ Say among the heathen that the Lord reigneth:
   the world also shall be established
      that it shall not be moved:
   he shall judge the people righteously.
¹¹ Let the heavens rejoice, and let the earth be glad;
   let the sea roar, and the fulness thereof.
¹² Let the field be joyful, and all that is therein;
   then shall all the trees of the wood rejoice
¹³ before the Lord; for he cometh,
   for he cometh to judge the earth:

he shall judge the world with righteousness,
and the people with his truth.

97

The Lord reigneth; let the earth rejoice;
let the multitude of isles be glad thereof.
2 Clouds and darkness are round about him:
righteousness and judgment are the habitation
of his throne.
3 A fire goeth before him,
and burneth up his enemies round about.
4 His lightnings enlightened the world:
the earth saw, and trembled.
5 The hills melted like wax at the presence of the Lord,
at the presence of the Lord of the whole earth.
6 The heavens declare his righteousness,
and all the people see his glory.
7 Confounded be all they that serve graven images,
that boast themselves of idols:
worship him, all ye gods.
8 Zion heard, and was glad;
and the daughters of Judah rejoiced
because of thy judgments, O Lord.
9 For thou, Lord, art high above all the earth:
thou art exalted far above all gods.
10 Ye that love the Lord, hate evil;
he preserveth the souls of his saints;
he delivereth them out of the hand
of the wicked.

¹¹ Light is sown for the righteous,
and gladness for the upright in heart.
¹² Rejoice in the Lord, ye righteous;
and give thanks at the remembrance
of his holiness.

98

A psalm.

O sing unto the Lord a new song;
for he hath done marvellous things:
his right hand, and his holy arm,
hath gotten him the victory.
² The Lord hath made known his salvation:
his righteousness hath he openly shewed
in the sight of the heathen.
³ He hath remembered his mercy and his truth
toward the house of Israel:
all the ends of the earth have seen
the salvation of our God.
⁴ Make a joyful noise unto the Lord,
all the earth: make a loud noise,
and rejoice, and sing praise.
⁵ Sing unto the Lord with the harp;
with the harp, and the voice of a psalm.
⁶ With trumpets and sound of cornet
make a joyful noise before the Lord, the King.
⁷ Let the sea roar, and the fulness thereof;

the world, and they that dwell therein.
⁸ Let the floods clap their hands;
    let the hills be joyful together
⁹ Before the Lord; for he cometh to judge the earth;
    with righteousness shall he judge the world,
        and the people with equity.

99 The Lord reigneth; let the people tremble:
    he sitteth between the cherubims;
        let the earth be moved.
² The Lord is great in Zion;
    and he is high above all the people.
³ Let them praise thy great and terrible name;
    for it is holy.
⁴ The king's strength also loveth judgment;
    thou dost establish equity,
        thou executest judgment
    and righteousness in Jacob.
⁵ Exalt ye the Lord our God,
    and worship at his footstool; for he is holy.
⁶ Moses and Aaron among his priests,
    and Samuel among them that call upon his name;
        they called upon the Lord,
    and he answered them.
⁷ He spake unto them in the cloudy pillar:
    they kept his testimonies,
        and the ordinance that he gave them.

⁸Thou answeredst them, O Lord our God:
  thou wast a God that forgavest them,
    though thou tookest vengeance of their inven-
    tions.
⁹Exalt the Lord our God, and worship at his holy
  hill; for the Lord our God is holy.

100 A psalm of praise.

Make a joyful noise unto the Lord, all ye lands.
²Serve the Lord with gladness:
  come before his presence with singing.
³Know ye that the Lord he is God;
  it is he that hath made us, and not we ourselves;
    we are his people,
  and the sheep of his pasture.
⁴Enter into his gates with thanksgiving,
  and into his courts with praise:
    be thankful unto him, and bless his name.
⁵For the Lord is good; his mercy is everlasting;
  and his truth endureth to all generations.

101 A psalm of David.

I will sing of mercy and judgment:
  unto thee, O Lord, will I sing.
²I will behave myself wisely in a perfect way.
  O when wilt thou come unto me?

I will walk within my house
with a perfect heart.
³ I will set no wicked thing before mine eyes;
I hate the work of them that turn aside;
it shall not cleave to me.
⁴A froward heart shall depart from me:
I will not know a wicked person.
⁵ Whoso privily slandereth his neighbour,
him will I cut off:
him that hath an high look
and a proud heart will not I suffer.
⁶ Mine eyes shall be upon the faithful of the land,
that they may dwell with me:
he that walketh in a perfect way,
he shall serve me.
⁷ He that worketh deceit shall not dwell
within my house:
he that telleth lies shall not tarry in my sight.
⁸ I will early destroy all the wicked of the land;
that I may cut off all wicked doers
from the city of the Lord.

102 A prayer of the afflicted, when he is overwhelmed, and poureth out his complaint before the Lord.

Hear my prayer, O Lord,
and let my cry come unto thee.

² Hide not thy face from me in the day
when I am in trouble; incline thine ear unto me:
in the day when I call answer me speedily.
³ For my days are consumed like smoke,
and my bones are burned as an hearth.
⁴ My heart is smitten, and withered like grass;
so that I forget to eat my bread.
⁵ By reason of the voice of my groaning my bones
cleave to my skin.
⁶ I am like a pelican of the wilderness:
I am like an owl of the desert.
⁷ I watch, and am as a sparrow
alone upon the house top.
⁸ Mine enemies reproach me all the day;
and they that are mad against me are sworn
against me.
⁹ For I have eaten ashes like bread,
and mingled my drink with weeping,
¹⁰ because of thine indignation and thy wrath;
for thou hast lifted me up, and cast me down.
¹¹ My days are like a shadow that declineth;
and I am withered like grass.
¹² But thou, O Lord, shalt endure for ever;
and thy remembrance unto all generations.
¹³ Thou shalt arise, and have mercy upon Zion;
for the time to favour her, yea,
the set time, is come.
¹⁴ For thy servants take pleasure in her stones,
and favour the dust thereof.

¹⁵ So the heathen shall fear the name of the Lord,
and all the kings of the earth thy glory.
¹⁶ When the Lord shall build up Zion,
he shall appear in his glory.
¹⁷ He will regard the prayer of the destitute,
and not despise their prayer.
¹⁸ This shall be written for the generation to come;
and the people which shall be created
shall praise the Lord.
¹⁹ For he hath looked down from the height
of his sanctuary;
from heaven did the Lord behold the earth;
²⁰ to hear the groaning of the prisoner;
to loose those that are appointed to death;
²¹ to declare the name of the Lord in Zion,
and his praise in Jerusalem;
²² when the people are gathered together,
and the kingdoms, to serve the Lord.
²³ He weakened my strength in the way;
he shortened my days.
²⁴ I said, 'O my God, take me not away
in the midst of my days;
thy years are throughout all generations.'
²⁵ Of old hast thou laid the foundation of the earth;
and the heavens are the work of thy hands.
²⁶ They shall perish, but thou shalt endure:
yea, all of them shall wax old like a garment;
as a vesture shalt thou change them,
and they shall be changed;

²⁷ but thou art the same,
  and thy years shall have no end.
²⁸ The children of thy servants shall continue,
  and their seed shall be established before thee.

103

A psalm of David.

Bless the Lord, O my soul;
  and all that is within me, bless his holy name.
² Bless the Lord, O my soul,
  and forget not all his benefits;
³ who forgiveth all thine iniquities;
  who healeth all thy diseases;
⁴ who redeemeth thy life from destruction;
  who crowneth thee with lovingkindness
    and tender mercies;
⁵ who satisfieth thy mouth with good things;
  so that thy youth is renewed like the eagle's.
⁶ The Lord executeth righteousness
  and judgment for all that are oppressed.
⁷ He made known his ways unto Moses,
  his acts unto the children of Israel.
⁸ The Lord is merciful and gracious,
  slow to anger, and plenteous in mercy.
⁹ He will not always chide;
  neither will he keep his anger for ever.
¹⁰ He hath not dealt with us after our sins;
  nor rewarded us according to our iniquities.

¹¹ For as the heaven is high above the earth,
　　so great is his mercy toward them that fear him.
¹² As far as the east is from the west,
　　so far hath he removed our transgressions
　　　　from us.
¹³ Like as a father pitieth his children,
　　so the Lord pitieth them that fear him.
¹⁴ For he knoweth our frame;
　　he remembereth that we are dust.
¹⁵ As for man, his days are as grass:
　　as a flower of the field, so he flourisheth.
¹⁶ For the wind passeth over it, and it is gone;
　　and the place thereof shall know it no more.
¹⁷ But the mercy of the Lord is from everlasting
　　to everlasting upon them that fear him,
　　　　and his righteousness unto children's children;
¹⁸ to such as keep his covenant,
　　and to those that remember his commandments
　　　　to do them.
¹⁹ The Lord hath prepared his throne in the heavens;
　　and his kingdom ruleth over all.
²⁰ Bless the Lord, ye his angels, that excel in strength,
　　that do his commandments,
　　　　hearkening unto the voice of his word.
²¹ Bless ye the Lord, all ye his hosts;
　　ye ministers of his, that do his pleasure.
²² Bless the Lord, all his works in all places
　　of his dominion: bless the Lord, O my soul.

104

Bless the Lord, O my soul.
O Lord my God, thou art very great;
  thou art clothed with honour and majesty.
2 Who coverest thyself with light as with a garment;
  who stretchest out the heavens like a curtain;
3 who layeth the beams of his chambers
  in the waters;
    who maketh the clouds his chariot;
  who walketh upon the wings of the wind;
4 who maketh his angels spirits;
  his ministers a flaming fire;
5 who laid the foundations of the earth,
  that it should not be removed for ever.
6 Thou coveredst it with the deep as with a garment:
  the waters stood above the mountains.
7 At thy rebuke they fled;
  at the voice of thy thunder they hasted away.
8 They go up by the mountains;
  they go down by the valleys unto the place
    which thou hast founded for them.
9 Thou hast set a bound that they may not pass over;
  that they turn not again to cover the earth.
10 He sendeth the springs into the valleys,
  which run among the hills.
11 They give drink to every beast of the field:
  the wild asses quench their thirst.
12 By them shall the fowls of the heaven
  have their habitation,

which sing among the branches.

¹³ He watereth the hills from his chambers:

the earth is satisfied with the fruit of thy works.

¹⁴ He causeth the grass to grow for the cattle,

and herb for the service of man,

that he may bring forth food out of the earth;

¹⁵ and wine that maketh glad the heart of man,

and oil to make his face to shine,

and bread which strengtheneth man's heart.

¹⁶ The trees of the Lord are full of sap;

the cedars of Lebanon, which he hath planted;

¹⁷ where the birds make their nests:

as for the stork, the fir trees are her house.

¹⁸ The high hills are a refuge for the wild goats;

and the rocks for the conies.

¹⁹ He appointed the moon for seasons;

the sun knoweth his going down.

²⁰ Thou makest darkness, and it is night;

wherein all the beasts of the forest do creep forth.

²¹ The young lions roar after their prey,

and seek their meat from God.

²² The sun ariseth, they gather themselves together,

and lay them down in their dens.

²³ Man goeth forth unto his work and to his labour

until the evening.

²⁴ O Lord, how manifold are thy works!

In wisdom hast thou made them all;

the earth is full of thy riches.

²⁵ So is this great and wide sea,
>   wherein are things creeping innumerable,
>   both small and great beasts.
²⁶ There go the ships;
>   there is that leviathan,
>   whom thou hast made to play therein.
²⁷ These wait all upon thee,
>   that thou mayest give them their meat
>   in due season.
²⁸ That thou givest them they gather:
>   thou openest thine hand,
>   they are filled with good.
²⁹ Thou hidest thy face, they are troubled:
>   thou takest away their breath,
>   they die, and return to their dust.
³⁰ Thou sendest forth thy spirit, they are created:
>   and thou renewest the face of the earth.
³¹ The glory of the Lord shall endure for ever:
>   the Lord shall rejoice in his works.
³² He looketh on the earth, and it trembleth:
>   he toucheth the hills, and they smoke.
³³ I will sing unto the Lord as long as I live:
>   I will sing praise to my God
>   while I have my being.
³⁴ My meditation of him shall be sweet:
>   I will be glad in the Lord.
³⁵ Let the sinners be consumed out of the earth,
>   and let the wicked be no more.

Bless thou the Lord, O my soul.
Praise ye the Lord.

105 O give thanks unto the Lord;
call upon his name;
make known his deeds among the people.
² Sing unto him, sing psalms unto him;
talk ye of all his wondrous works.
³ Glory ye in his holy name;
let the heart of them rejoice that seek the Lord.
⁴ Seek the Lord, and his strength;
seek his face evermore.
⁵ Remember his marvellous works that he hath done;
his wonders, and the judgments of his mouth;
⁶ O ye seed of Abraham his servant,
ye children of Jacob his chosen.
⁷ He is the Lord our God;
his judgments are in all the earth.
⁸ He hath remembered his covenant for ever,
the word which he commanded
to a thousand generations.
⁹ Which covenant he made with Abraham,
and his oath unto Isaac;
¹⁰ and confirmed the same unto Jacob for a law,
and to Israel for an everlasting covenant,
¹¹ saying, 'Unto thee will I give the land of Canaan,
the lot of your inheritance,'

¹² when they were but a few men in number;
   yea, very few, and strangers in it.
¹³ When they went from one nation to another,
   from one kingdom to another people;
¹⁴ he suffered no man to do them wrong:
   yea, he reproved kings for their sakes,
¹⁵ saying, 'Touch not mine anointed,
   and do my prophets no harm.'
¹⁶ Moreover he called for a famine upon the land:
   he brake the whole staff of bread.
¹⁷ He sent a man before them,
   even Joseph, who was sold for a servant,
¹⁸ whose feet they hurt with fetters:
   he was laid in iron:
¹⁹ until the time that his word came:
   the word of the Lord tried him.
²⁰ The king sent and loosed him;
   even the ruler of the people, and let him go free.
²¹ He made him lord of his house,
   and ruler of all his substance:
²² to bind his princes at his pleasure;
   and teach his senators wisdom.
²³ Israel also came into Egypt;
   and Jacob sojourned in the land of Ham.
²⁴ And he increased his people greatly;
   and made them stronger than their enemies.
²⁵ He turned their heart to hate his people,
   to deal subtilly with his servants.

²⁶ He sent Moses his servant;
   and Aaron whom he had chosen.
²⁷ They shewed his signs among them,
   and wonders in the land of Ham.
²⁸ He sent darkness, and made it dark;
   and they rebelled not against his word.
²⁹ He turned their waters into blood,
   and slew their fish.
³⁰ Their land brought forth frogs in abundance,
   in the chambers of their kings.
³¹ He spake, and there came divers sorts of flies,
   and lice in all their coasts.
³² He gave them hail for rain,
   and flaming fire in their land.
³³ He smote their vines also and their fig trees;
   and brake the trees of their coasts.
³⁴ He spake, and the locusts came,
   and caterpillers, and that without number,
³⁵ and did eat up all the herbs in their land,
   and devoured the fruit of their ground.
³⁶ He smote also all the firstborn in their land,
   the chief of all their strength.
³⁷ He brought them forth also with silver and gold;
   and there was not one feeble person
      among their tribes.
³⁸ Egypt was glad when they departed,
   for the fear of them fell upon them.
³⁹ He spread a cloud for a covering;
   and fire to give light in the night.

⁴⁰ The people asked, and he brought quails,
and satisfied them with the bread of heaven.
⁴¹ He opened the rock, and the waters gushed out;
they ran in the dry places like a river.
⁴² For he remembered his holy promise,
and Abraham his servant.
⁴³ And he brought forth his people with joy,
and his chosen with gladness;
⁴⁴ and gave them the lands of the heathen;
and they inherited the labour of the people;
⁴⁵ that they might observe his statutes,
and keep his laws. Praise ye the Lord.

106

Praise ye the Lord.
O give thanks unto the Lord; for he is good;
for his mercy endureth for ever.
² Who can utter the mighty acts of the Lord?
Who can shew forth all his praise?
³ Blessed are they that keep judgment,
and he that doeth righteousness at all times.
⁴ Remember me, O Lord, with the favour
that thou bearest unto thy people:
O visit me with thy salvation,
⁵ that I may see the good of thy chosen,
that I may rejoice in the gladness of thy nation,
that I may glory with thine inheritance.
⁶ We have sinned with our fathers,

we have committed iniquity,
   we have done wickedly.
⁷Our fathers understood not thy wonders in Egypt;
   they remembered not the multitude
      of thy mercies;
   but provoked him at the sea,
      even at the Red sea.
⁸Nevertheless he saved them for his name's sake,
   that he might make his mighty power
      to be known.
⁹He rebuked the Red sea also, and it was dried up:
   so he led them through the depths,
      as through the wilderness.
¹⁰And he saved them from the hand of him
   that hated them, and redeemed them
      from the hand of the enemy.
¹¹And the waters covered their enemies:
   there was not one of them left.
¹²Then believed they his words;
   they sang his praise.
¹³They soon forgat his works;
   they waited not for his counsel,
¹⁴but lusted exceedingly in the wilderness,
   and tempted God in the desert.
¹⁵And he gave them their request;
   but sent leanness into their soul.
¹⁶They envied Moses also in the camp,
   and Aaron the saint of the Lord.

¹⁷ The earth opened and swallowed up Dathan,
and covered the company of Abiram.
¹⁸ And a fire was kindled in their company;
the flame burned up the wicked.
¹⁹ They made a calf in Horeb,
and worshipped the molten image.
²⁰ Thus they changed their glory
into the similitude of an ox that eateth grass.
²¹ They forgat God their saviour,
which had done great things in Egypt;
²² wondrous works in the land of Ham,
and terrible things by the Red sea.
²³ Therefore he said that he would destroy them,
had not Moses his chosen stood before him
in the breach, to turn away his wrath,
lest he should destroy them.
²⁴ Yea, they despised the pleasant land,
they believed not his word,
²⁵ but murmured in their tents,
and hearkened not unto the voice of the Lord.
²⁶ Therefore he lifted up his hand against them,
to overthrow them in the wilderness,
²⁷ to overthrow their seed also among the nations,
and to scatter them in the lands.
²⁸ They joined themselves also unto Baal-peor,
and ate the sacrifices of the dead.
²⁹ Thus they provoked him to anger
with their inventions;
and the plague brake in upon them.

³⁰ Then stood up Phinehas, and executed judgment;
and so the plague was stayed.
³¹ And that was counted unto him for righteousness
unto all generations for evermore.
³² They angered him also at the waters of strife,
so that it went ill with Moses for their sakes,
³³ because they provoked his spirit,
so that he spake unadvisedly with his lips.
³⁴ They did not destroy the nations,
concerning whom the Lord commanded them;
³⁵ but were mingled among the heathen,
and learned their works.
³⁶ And they served their idols,
which were a snare unto them.
³⁷ Yea, they sacrificed their sons
and their daughters unto devils,
³⁸ and shed innocent blood,
even the blood of their sons
and of their daughters,
whom they sacrificed unto the idols of Canaan;
and the land was polluted with blood.
³⁹ Thus were they defiled with their own works,
and went a whoring with their own inventions.
⁴⁰ Therefore was the wrath of the Lord
kindled against his people, insomuch
that he abhorred his own inheritance.
⁴¹ And he gave them into the hand of the heathen;
and they that hated them ruled over them.

⁴² Their enemies also oppressed them,
    and they were brought into subjection
        under their hand.
⁴³ Many times did he deliver them;
    but they provoked him with their counsel,
        and were brought low for their iniquity.
⁴⁴ Nevertheless he regarded their affliction,
    when he heard their cry;
⁴⁵ and he remembered for them his covenant,
    and repented according to the multitude
        of his mercies.
⁴⁶ He made them also to be pitied of all those
    that carried them captives.
⁴⁷ Save us, O Lord our God,
    and gather us from among the heathen,
        to give thanks unto thy holy name,
    and to triumph in thy praise.
⁴⁸ Blessed be the Lord God of Israel from everlasting
    to everlasting;
        and let all the people say, 'Amen.'
    Praise ye the Lord.

107

O Give thanks unto the Lord,
    for he is good, for his mercy endureth for ever.
² Let the redeemed of the Lord say so,
    whom he hath redeemed from the hand
        of the enemy;

³and gathered them out of the lands,
> from the east, and from the west,
>> from the north, and from the south.
⁴They wandered in the wilderness in a solitary way;
> they found no city to dwell in.
⁵Hungry and thirsty,
> their soul fainted in them.
⁶Then they cried unto the Lord in their trouble,
> and he delivered them out of their distresses.
⁷And he led them forth by the right way,
> that they might go to a city of habitation.
⁸Oh that men would praise the Lord
> for his goodness,
>> and for his wonderful works
> to the children of men!
⁹For he satisfieth the longing soul,
> and filleth the hungry soul with goodness.
¹⁰Such as sit in darkness and in the shadow of death,
> being bound in affliction and iron,
¹¹because they rebelled against the words of God,
> and contemned the counsel of the most High;
¹²therefore he brought down their heart with labour;
> they fell down, and there was none to help.
¹³Then they cried unto the Lord in their trouble,
> and he saved them out of their distresses.
¹⁴He brought them out of darkness
> and the shadow of death,
>> and brake their bands in sunder.

¹⁵ Oh that men would praise the Lord
for his goodness, and for his wonderful works
to the children of men!
¹⁶ For he hath broken the gates of brass,
and cut the bars of iron in sunder.
¹⁷ Fools because of their transgression,
and because of their iniquities, are afflicted.
¹⁸ Their soul abhorreth all manner of meat;
and they draw near unto the gates of death.
¹⁹ Then they cry unto the Lord in their trouble,
and he saveth them out of their distresses.
²⁰ He sent his word, and healed them,
and delivered them from their destructions.
²¹ Oh that men would praise the Lord
for his goodness, and for his wonderful works
to the children of men!
²² And let them sacrifice the sacrifices
of thanksgiving,
and declare his works with rejoicing.
²³ They that go down to the sea in ships,
that do business in great waters;
²⁴ these see the works of the Lord,
and his wonders in the deep.
²⁵ For he commandeth, and raiseth the stormy wind,
which lifteth up the waves thereof.
²⁶ They mount up to the heaven,
they go down again to the depths:
their soul is melted because of trouble.

²⁷ They reel to and fro, and stagger
   like a drunken man, and are at their wits' end.
²⁸ Then they cry unto the Lord in their trouble,
   and he bringeth them out of their distresses.
²⁹ He maketh the storm a calm,
   so that the waves thereof are still.
³⁰ Then are they glad because they be quiet;
   so he bringeth them unto their desired haven.
³¹ Oh that men would praise the Lord
   for his goodness, and for his wonderful works
      to the children of men!
³² Let them exalt him also in the congregation
   of the people, and praise him
      in the assembly of the elders.
³³ He turneth rivers into a wilderness,
   and the watersprings into dry ground,
³⁴ a fruitful land into barrenness,
   for the wickedness of them that dwell therein.
³⁵ He turneth the wilderness into a standing water,
   and dry ground into watersprings.
³⁶ And there he maketh the hungry to dwell,
   that they may prepare a city for habitation,
³⁷ and sow the fields, and plant vineyards,
   which may yield fruits of increase.
³⁸ He blesseth them also,
   so that they are multiplied greatly;
      and suffereth not their cattle to decrease.
³⁹ Again, they are minished and brought low
   through oppression, affliction, and sorrow.

⁴⁰ He poureth contempt upon princes,
>> and causeth them to wander in the wilderness,
>>> where there is no way.
⁴¹ Yet setteth he the poor on high from affliction,
>> and maketh him families like a flock.
⁴² The righteous shall see it, and rejoice;
>> and all inquity shall stop her mouth.
⁴³ Whoso is wise, and will observe these things,
>> even they shall understand the lovingkindness
>>> of the Lord.

108

A song or psalm of David.

O God, my heart is fixed;
I will sing and give praise, even with my glory.
² Awake, psaltery and harp:
>> I myself will awake early.
³ I will praise thee, O Lord, among the people;
>> and I will sing praises unto thee
>>> among the nations.
⁴ For thy mercy is great above the heavens;
>> and thy truth reacheth unto the clouds.
⁵ Be thou exalted, O God, above the heavens;
>> and thy glory above all the earth,
⁶ that thy beloved may be delivered:
>> save with thy right hand, and answer me.
⁷ God hath spoken in his holiness;
>> I will rejoice, I will divide Shechem,
>>> and mete out the valley of Succoth.

8 Gilead is mine; Manasseh is mine;
    Ephraim also is the strength of mine head;
        Judah is my lawgiver;
9 Moab is my washpot;
    over Edom will I cast out my shoe;
        over Philistia will I triumph.
10 Who will bring me into the strong city?
    Who will lead me into Edom?
11 Wilt not thou, O God, who hast cast us off?
    And wilt not thou, O God, go forth
        with our hosts?
12 Give us help from trouble;
    for vain is the help of man.
13 Through God we shall do valiantly;
    for he it is that shall tread down our enemies.

109 To the chief musician, a psalm of David.

Hold not thy peace, O God of my praise;
2 for the mouth of the wicked and the mouth of the
    deceitful are opened against me:
        they have spoken against me
    with a lying tongue.
3 They compassed me about also
    with words of hatred;
        and fought against me without a cause.
4 For my love they are my adversaries;
    but I give myself unto prayer.

⁵And they have rewarded me evil for good,
    and hatred for my love.
⁶Set thou a wicked man over him;
    and let Satan stand at his right hand.
⁷When he shall be judged,
    let him be condemned;
        and let his prayer become sin.
⁸Let his days be few;
    and let another take his office.
⁹Let his children be fatherless;
    and his wife a widow.
¹⁰Let his children be continually vagabonds, and beg;
    let them seek their bread also
        out of their desolate places.
¹¹Let the extortioner catch all that he hath;
    and let the strangers spoil his labour.
¹²Let there be none to extend mercy unto him:
    neither let there be any to favour
        his fatherless children.
¹³Let his posterity be cut off;
    and in the generation following
        let their name be blotted out.
¹⁴Let the iniquity of his fathers be remembered
    with the Lord;
        and let not the sin of his mother
    be blotted out.
¹⁵Let them be before the Lord continually,
    that he may cut off the memory of them
        from the earth.

¹⁶ Because that he remembered not to shew mercy,
>   but persecuted the poor and needy man,
>   that he might even slay the broken in heart.
¹⁷ As he loved cursing, so let it come unto him:
>   as he delighted not in blessing,
>   so let it be far from him.
¹⁸ As he clothed himself with cursing like
>   as with his garment,
>   so let it come into his bowels like water,
>   and like oil into his bones.
¹⁹ Let it be unto him as the garment
>   which covereth him,
>   and for a girdle wherewith
>   he is girded continually.
²⁰ Let this be the reward of mine adversaries
>   from the Lord,
>   and of them that speak evil against my soul.
²¹ But do thou for me, O God the Lord,
>   for thy name's sake,
>   because thy mercy is good, deliver thou me.
²² For I am poor and needy,
>   and my heart is wounded within me.
²³ I am gone like the shadow when it declineth:
>   I am tossed up and down as the locust.
²⁴ My knees are weak through fasting;
>   and my flesh faileth of fatness.
²⁵ I became also a reproach unto them;
>   when they looked upon me
>   they shaked their heads.

²⁶ Help me, O Lord my God:
O save me according to thy mercy,
²⁷ that they may know that this is thy hand;
that thou, Lord, hast done it.
²⁸ Let them curse, but bless thou:
when they arise, let them be ashamed;
but let thy servant rejoice.
²⁹ Let mine adversaries be clothed with shame,
and let them cover themselves
with their own confusion, as with a mantle.
³⁰ I will greatly praise the Lord with my mouth;
yea, I will praise him among the multitude.
³¹ For he shall stand at the right hand of the poor,
to save him from those that condemn his soul.

110

A psalm of David.

The Lord said unto my Lord,
'Sit thou at my right hand,
until I make thine enemies thy footstool.'
² The Lord shall send the rod of thy strength
out of Zion: rule thou in the midst
of thine enemies.
³ Thy people shall be willing in the day of thy power,
in the beauties of holiness from the womb
of the morning:
thou hast the dew of thy youth.
⁴ The Lord hath sworn, and will not repent,

'Thou art a priest for ever after
  the order of Melchizedek.'
⁵ The Lord at thy right hand
  shall strike through kings in the day of his wrath.
⁶ He shall judge among the heathen,
  he shall fill the places with the dead bodies;
    he shall wound the heads over many countries.
⁷ He shall drink of the brook in the way;
  therefore shall he lift up the head.

111 Praise ye the Lord.
  I will praise the Lord with my whole heart,
    in the assembly of the upright,
  and in the congregation.
² The works of the Lord are great, sought out
  of all them that have pleasure therein.
³ His work is honourable and glorious;
  and his righteousness endureth for ever.
⁴ He hath made his wonderful works
  to be remembered:
    the Lord is gracious and full of compassion.
⁵ He hath given meat unto them that fear him:
  he will ever be mindful of his covenant.
⁶ He hath shewed his people the power of his works,
  that he may give them the heritage
    of the heathen.
⁷ The works of his hands are verity and judgment;
  all his commandments are sure.

⁸ They stand fast for ever and ever,
　　and are done in truth and uprightness.
⁹ He sent redemption unto his people:
　　he hath commanded his covenant for ever:
　　　　holy and reverend is his name.
¹⁰ The fear of the Lord is the beginning of wisdom:
　　a good understanding have all they
　　　　that do his commandments:
　　his praise endureth for ever.

112 Praise ye the Lord.
　　Blessed is the man that feareth the Lord,
　　　　that delighteth greatly in his commandments.
² His seed shall be mighty upon earth:
　　the generation of the upright shall be blessed.
³ Wealth and riches shall be in his house;
　　and his righteousness endureth for ever.
⁴ Unto the upright there ariseth light in the darkness:
　　he is gracious, and full of compassion,
　　　　and righteous.
⁵ A good man sheweth favour, and lendeth:
　　he will guide his affairs with discretion.
⁶ Surely he shall not be moved for ever:
　　the righteous shall be in everlasting
　　　　remembrance.
⁷ He shall not be afraid of evil tidings:
　　his heart is fixed, trusting in the Lord.

⁸ His heart is established, he shall not be afraid,
    until he see his desire
        upon his enemies.
⁹ He hath dispersed, he hath given to the poor;
    his righteousness endureth for ever;
        his horn shall be exalted with honour.
¹⁰ The wicked shall see it, and be grieved;
    he shall gnash with his teeth, and melt away:
        the desire of the wicked shall perish.

113 Praise ye the Lord.
    Praise, O ye servants of the Lord,
        praise the name of the Lord.
² Blessed be the name of the Lord
    from this time forth and for evermore.
³ From the rising of the sun unto the going down
    of the same the Lord's name is to be praised.
⁴ The Lord is high above all nations,
    and his glory above the heavens.
⁵ Who is like unto the Lord our God,
    who dwelleth on high,
⁶ who humbleth himself to behold the things
    that are in heaven, and in the earth!
⁷ He raiseth up the poor out of the dust,
    and lifteth the needy out of the dunghill,
⁸ that he may set him with princes,
    even with the princes of his people.

⁹ He maketh the barren woman to keep house,
and to be a joyful mother of children.
Praise ye the Lord.

114 When Israel went out of Egypt,
the house of Jacob from a people
of strange language,
² Judah was his sanctuary,
and Israel his dominion.
³ The sea saw it, and fled:
Jordan was driven back.
⁴ The mountains skipped like rams,
and the little hills like lambs.
⁵ What ailed thee, O thou sea, that thou fleddest?
Thou Jordan, that thou wast driven back?
⁶ Ye mountains, that ye skipped like rams;
and ye little hills, like lambs?
⁷ Tremble, thou earth, at the presence of the Lord,
at the presence of the God of Jacob,
⁸ which turned the rock into a standing water,
the flint into a fountain of waters.

115 Not unto us, O Lord, not unto us,
but unto thy name give glory, for thy mercy,
and for thy truth's sake.
² Wherefore should the heathen say,
'Where is now their God?'
³ But our God is in the heavens:

he hath done whatsoever he hath pleased.
⁴ Their idols are silver and gold,
   the work of men's hands.
⁵ They have mouths, but they speak not:
   eyes have they, but they see not:
⁶ they have ears, but they hear not:
   noses have they, but they smell not:
⁷ they have hands, but they handle not:
   feet have they, but they walk not:
      neither speak they through their throat.
⁸ They that make them are like unto them;
   so is every one that trusteth in them.
⁹ O Israel, trust thou in the Lord:
   he is their help and their shield.
¹⁰ O house of Aaron, trust in the Lord:
   he is their help and their shield.
¹¹ Ye that fear the Lord; trust in the Lord:
   he is their help and their shield.
¹² The Lord hath been mindful of us:
   he will bless us;
      he will bless the house of Israel;
   he will bless the house of Aaron.
¹³ He will bless them that fear the Lord,
   both small and great.
¹⁴ The Lord shall increase you more and more,
   you and your children.
¹⁵ Ye are blessed of the Lord
   which made heaven and earth.

¹⁶ The heaven, even the heavens, are the Lord's:
     but the earth hath he given to the children
        of men.
¹⁷ The dead praise not the Lord,
     neither any that go down into silence.
¹⁸ But we will bless the Lord from this time forth
     and for evermore. Praise the Lord.

116   I love the Lord, because he hath heard
     my voice and my supplications.
² Because he hath inclined his ear unto me,
     therefore will I call upon him as long as I live.
³ The sorrows of death compassed me,
     and the pains of hell gat hold upon me:
        I found trouble and sorrow.
⁴ Then called I upon the name of the Lord:
     'O Lord, I beseech thee, deliver my soul.'
⁵ Gracious is the Lord, and righteous;
     yea, our God is merciful.
⁶ The Lord preserveth the simple:
     I was brought low, and he helped me.
⁷ Return unto thy rest, O my soul;
     for the Lord hath dealt bountifully with thee.
⁸ For thou hast delivered my soul from death,
     mine eyes from tears, and my feet from falling.
⁹ I will walk before the Lord
     in the land of the living.

¹⁰ I believed, therefore have I spoken:
    I was greatly afflicted:
¹¹ I said in my haste, 'All men are liars.'
¹² What shall I render unto the Lord
    for all his benefits toward me?
¹³ I will take the cup of salvation,
    and call upon the name of the Lord.
¹⁴ I will pay my vows unto the Lord
    now in the presence of all his people.
¹⁵ Precious in the sight of the Lord
    is the death of his saints.
¹⁶ O Lord, truly I am thy servant;
    I am thy servant, and the son of thine handmaid:
        thou hast loosed my bonds.
¹⁷ I will offer to thee the sacrifice of thanksgiving,
    and will call upon the name of the Lord.
¹⁸ I will pay my vows unto the Lord,
    now in the presence of all his people,
¹⁹ in the courts of the Lord's house,
    in the midst of thee, O Jerusalem.
        Praise ye the Lord.

117   O praise the Lord, all ye nations:
      praise him, all ye people.
² For his merciful kindness is great toward us:
    and the truth of the Lord endureth for ever.
        Praise ye the Lord.

118

O give thanks unto the Lord; for he is good,
because his mercy endureth for ever.

² Let Israel now say
that his mercy endureth for ever.

³ Let the house of Aaron now say
that his mercy endureth for ever.

⁴ Let them now that fear the Lord say
that his mercy endureth for ever.

⁵ I called upon the Lord in distress:
the Lord answered me,
and set me in a large place.

⁶ The Lord is on my side;
I will not fear: what can man do unto me?

⁷ The Lord taketh my part with them that help me;
therefore shall I see my desire
upon them that hate me.

⁸ It is better to trust in the Lord
than to put confidence in man.

⁹ It is better to trust in the Lord
than to put confidence in princes.

¹⁰ All nations compassed me about;
but in the name of the Lord will I destroy them.

¹¹ They compassed me about;
yea, they compassed me about;
but in the name of the Lord I will destroy them.

¹² They compassed me about like bees;
they are quenched as the fire of thorns,
for in the name of the Lord

I will destroy them.

¹³ Thou hast thrust sore at me that I might fall;
 but the Lord helped me.

¹⁴ The Lord is my strength and song,
 and is become my salvation.

¹⁵ The voice of rejoicing and salvation is in the
 tabernacles of the righteous:
  the right hand of the Lord doeth valiantly.

¹⁶ The right hand of the Lord is exalted:
 the right hand of the Lord doeth valiantly.

¹⁷ I shall not die, but live,
 and declare the works of the Lord.

¹⁸ The Lord hath chastened me sore;
 but he hath not given me over unto death.

¹⁹ Open to me the gates of righteousness:
 I will go into them, and I will praise the Lord:

²⁰ this gate of the Lord, into which
 the righteous shall enter.

²¹ I will praise thee; for thou hast heard me,
 and art become my salvation.

²² The stone which the builders refused
 is become the head stone of the corner.

²³ This is the Lord's doing;
 it is marvellous in our eyes.

²⁴ This is the day which the Lord hath made;
 we will rejoice and be glad in it.

²⁵ Save now, I beseech thee, O Lord:
 O Lord, I beseech thee, send now prosperity.

²⁶ Blessed be he that cometh in the name of the Lord:
  we have blessed you out of the house of the Lord.
²⁷ God is the Lord, which hath shewed us light:
  bind the sacrifice with cords, even unto the horns
    of the altar.
²⁸ Thou art my God, and I will praise thee:
  thou art my God, I will exalt thee.
²⁹ O give thanks unto the Lord; for he is good;
  for his mercy endureth for ever.

119

ALEPH

Blessed are the undefiled in the way,
  who walk in the law of the Lord.
² Blessed are they that keep his testimonies,
  and that seek him with the whole heart.
³ They also do no iniquity: they walk in his ways.
⁴ Thou hast commanded us to keep
  thy precepts diligently.
⁵ O that my ways were directed to keep thy statutes!
⁶ Then shall I not be ashamed,
  when I have respect unto all thy commandments.
⁷ I will praise thee with uprightness of heart,
  when I shall have learned
    thy righteous judgments.
⁸ I will keep thy statutes;
  O forsake me not utterly.

BETH

⁹ Wherewithal shall a young man cleanse his way?
  By taking heed thereto according to thy word.
¹⁰ With my whole heart have I sought thee;
  O let me not wander from thy commandments.
¹¹ Thy word have I hid in mine heart,
  that I might not sin against thee.
¹² Blessed art thou, O Lord: teach me thy statutes.
¹³ With my lips have I declared
  all the judgments of thy mouth.
¹⁴ I have rejoiced in the way of thy testimonies,
  as much as in all riches.
¹⁵ I will meditate in thy precepts,
  and have respect unto thy ways.
¹⁶ I will delight myself in thy statutes;
  I will not forget thy word.

GIMEL

¹⁷ Deal bountifully with thy servant,
  that I may live, and keep thy word.
¹⁸ Open thou mine eyes, that I may behold
  wondrous things out of thy law.
¹⁹ I am a stranger in the earth:
  hide not thy commandments from me.
²⁰ My soul breaketh for the longing that it hath unto
  thy judgments at all times.
²¹ Thou hast rebuked the proud that are cursed,
  which do err from thy commandments.

²² Remove from me reproach and contempt,
   for I have kept thy testimonies.
²³ Princes also did sit and speak against me;
   but thy servant did meditate in thy statutes.
²⁴ Thy testimonies also are my delight
   and my counsellors.

DALETH

²⁵ My soul cleaveth unto the dust;
   quicken thou me according to thy word.
²⁶ I have declared my ways, and thou heardest me:
   teach me thy statutes.
²⁷ Make me to understand the way of thy precepts;
   so shall I talk of thy wondrous works.
²⁸ My soul melteth for heaviness:
   strengthen thou me according unto thy word.
²⁹ Remove from me the way of lying;
   and grant me thy law graciously.
³⁰ I have chosen the way of truth:
   thy judgments have I laid before me.
³¹ I have stuck unto thy testimonies:
   O Lord, put me not to shame.
³² I will run the way of thy commandments,
   when thou shalt enlarge my heart.

HE

³³ Teach me, O Lord, the way of thy statutes;
   and I shall keep it unto the end.

³⁴ Give me understanding, and I shall keep thy law;
yea, I shall observe it with my whole heart.

³⁵ Make me to go in the path of thy commandments;
for therein do I delight.

³⁶ Incline my heart unto thy testimonies,
and not to covetousness.

³⁷ Turn away mine eyes from beholding vanity;
and quicken thou me in thy way.

³⁸ Stablish thy word unto thy servant,
who is devoted to thy fear.

³⁹ Turn away my reproach which I fear;
for thy judgments are good.

⁴⁰ Behold, I have longed after thy precepts:
quicken me in thy righteousness.

VAU

⁴¹ Let thy mercies come also unto me, O Lord,
even thy salvation, according to thy word.

⁴² So shall I have wherewith to answer him
that reproacheth me; for I trust in thy word.

⁴³ And take not the word of truth utterly
out of my mouth;
for I have hoped in thy judgments.

⁴⁴ So shall I keep thy law continually
for ever and ever.

⁴⁵ And I will walk at liberty; for I seek thy precepts.

⁴⁶ I will speak of thy testimonies also before kings,
and will not be ashamed.

⁴⁷And I will delight myself in thy commandments,
    which I have loved.
⁴⁸My hands also will I lift up
    unto thy commandments, which I have loved;
        and I will meditate in thy statutes.

ZAIN

⁴⁹Remember the word unto thy servant,
    upon which thou hast caused me to hope.
⁵⁰This is my comfort in my affliction;
    for thy word hath quickened me.
⁵¹The proud have had me greatly in derision;
    yet have I not declined from thy law.
⁵²I remembered thy judgments of old, O Lord;
    and have comforted myself.
⁵³Horror hath taken hold upon me
    because of the wicked that forsake thy law.
⁵⁴Thy statutes have been my songs
    in the house of my pilgrimage.
⁵⁵I have remembered thy name, O Lord,
    in the night, and have kept thy law.
⁵⁶This I had, because I kept thy precepts.

CHETH

⁵⁷Thou art my portion, O Lord:
    I have said that I would keep thy words.
⁵⁸I intreated thy favour with my whole heart:
    be merciful unto me according to thy word.

⁵⁹ I thought on my ways,
and turned my feet unto thy testimonies.
⁶⁰ I made haste,
and delayed not to keep thy commandments.
⁶¹ The bands of the wicked have robbed me;
but I have not forgotten thy law.
⁶² At midnight I will rise to give thanks unto thee
because of thy righteous judgments.
⁶³ I am a companion of all them that fear thee,
and of them that keep thy precepts.
⁶⁴ The earth, O Lord, is full of thy mercy:
teach me thy statutes.

TETH

⁶⁵ Thou hast dealt well with thy servant, O Lord,
according unto thy word.
⁶⁶ Teach me good judgment and knowledge;
for I have believed thy commandments.
⁶⁷ Before I was afflicted I went astray;
but now have I kept thy word.
⁶⁸ Thou art good, and doest good;
teach me thy statutes.
⁶⁹ The proud have forged a lie against me;
but I will keep thy precepts with my whole heart.
⁷⁰ Their heart is as fat as grease;
but I delight in thy law.
⁷¹ It is good for me that I have been afflicted;
that I might learn thy statutes.

⁷²The law of thy mouth is better unto me
　　than thousands of gold and silver.

JOD

⁷³Thy hands have made me and fashioned me:
　　give me understanding,
　　　　that I may learn thy commandments.
⁷⁴They that fear thee will be glad when they see me;
　　because I have hoped in thy word.
⁷⁵I know, O Lord, that thy judgments are right,
　　and that thou in faithfulness hast afflicted me.
⁷⁶Let, I pray thee, thy merciful kindness
　　be for my comfort,
　　　　according to thy word unto thy servant.
⁷⁷Let thy tender mercies come unto me,
　　that I may live; for thy law is my delight.
⁷⁸Let the proud be ashamed;
　　for they dealt perversely with me
　　　　without a cause;
　　but I will meditate in thy precepts.
⁷⁹Let those that fear thee turn unto me,
　　and those that have known thy testimonies.
⁸⁰Let my heart be sound in thy statutes;
　　that I be not ashamed.

CAPH

⁸¹My soul fainteth for thy salvation;
　　but I hope in thy word.

⁸² Mine eyes fail for thy word, saying,
'When wilt thou comfort me?'
⁸³ For I am become like a bottle in the smoke;
yet do I not forget thy statutes.
⁸⁴ How many are the days of thy servant?
When wilt thou execute judgment on them
that persecute me?
⁸⁵ The proud have digged pits for me,
which are not after thy law.
⁸⁶ All thy commandments are faithful;
they persecute me wrongfully;
help thou me.
⁸⁷ They had almost consumed me upon earth;
but I forsook not thy precepts.
⁸⁸ Quicken me after thy lovingkindness;
so shall I keep the testimony of thy mouth.

LAMED

⁸⁹ For ever, O Lord, thy word is settled in heaven.
⁹⁰ Thy faithfulness is unto all generations:
thou hast established the earth, and it abideth.
⁹¹ They continue this day according to
thine ordinances; for all are thy servants.
⁹² Unless thy law had been my delights,
I should then have perished in mine affliction.
⁹³ I will never forget thy precepts;
for with them thou hast quickened me.
⁹⁴ I am thine, save me;
for I have sought thy precepts.

⁹⁵ The wicked have waited for me to destroy me;
  but I will consider thy testimonies.
⁹⁶ I have seen an end of all perfection;
  but thy commandment is exceeding broad.

MEM

⁹⁷ O how love I thy law!
  It is my meditation all the day.
⁹⁸ Thou through thy commandments hast made
  me wiser than mine enemies;
    for they are ever with me.
⁹⁹ I have more understanding than all my teachers;
  for thy testimonies are my meditation.
¹⁰⁰ I understand more than the ancients,
  because I keep thy precepts.
¹⁰¹ I have refrained my feet from every evil way,
  that I might keep thy word.
¹⁰² I have not departed from thy judgments;
  for thou hast taught me.
¹⁰³ How sweet are thy words unto my taste!
  Yea, sweeter than honey to my mouth!
¹⁰⁴ Through thy precepts I get understanding;
  therefore I hate every false way.

NUN

¹⁰⁵ Thy word is a lamp unto my feet,
  and a light unto my path.
¹⁰⁶ I have sworn, and I will perform it,
  that I will keep thy righteous judgments.

[107] I am afflicted very much: quicken me, O Lord,
   according unto thy word.
[108] Accept, I beseech thee,
   the freewill offerings of my mouth, O Lord,
      and teach me thy judgments.
[109] My soul is continually in my hand;
   yet do I not forget thy law.
[110] The wicked have laid a snare for me;
   yet I erred not from thy precepts.
[111] Thy testimonies have I taken as an heritage for ever;
   for they are the rejoicing of my heart.
[112] I have inclined mine heart to perform thy statutes
   alway, even unto the end.

SAMECH

[113] I hate vain thoughts; but thy law do I love.
[114] Thou art my hiding place and my shield:
   I hope in thy word.
[115] Depart from me, ye evildoers;
   for I will keep the commandments of my God.
[116] Uphold me according unto thy word,
   that I may live;
      and let me not be ashamed of my hope.
[117] Hold thou me up, and I shall be safe;
   and I will have respect unto thy statutes
      continually.
[118] Thou hast trodden down all them that err
   from thy statutes; for their deceit is falsehood.

¹¹⁹ Thou puttest away all the wicked of the earth
   like dross; therefore I love thy testimonies.
¹²⁰ My flesh trembleth for fear of thee;
   and I am afraid of thy judgments.

AIN

¹²¹ I have done judgment and justice:
   leave me not to mine oppressors.
¹²² Be surety for thy servant for good:
   let not the proud oppress me.
¹²³ Mine eyes fail for thy salvation,
   and for the word of thy righteousness.
¹²⁴ Deal with thy servant according unto thy mercy,
   and teach me thy statutes.
¹²⁵ I am thy servant; give me understanding,
   that I may know thy testimonies.
¹²⁶ It is time for thee, Lord, to work;
   for they have made void thy law.
¹²⁷ Therefore I love thy commandments above gold;
   yea, above fine gold.
¹²⁸ Therefore I esteem all thy precepts concerning
   all things to be right;
      and I hate every false way.

PE

¹²⁹ Thy testimonies are wonderful;
   therefore doth my soul keep them.
¹³⁰ The entrance of thy words giveth light;

it giveth understanding unto the simple.
¹³¹ I opened my mouth, and panted;
   for I longed for thy commandments.
¹³² Look thou upon me, and be merciful unto me,
      as thou usest to do unto those
            that love thy name.
¹³³ Order my steps in thy word;
      and let not any iniquity have dominion over me.
¹³⁴ Deliver me from the oppression of man:
      so will I keep thy precepts.
¹³⁵ Make thy face to shine upon thy servant;
      and teach me thy statutes.
¹³⁶ Rivers of waters run down mine eyes,
      because they keep not thy law.

TZADDI

¹³⁷ Righteous art thou, O Lord,
      and upright are thy judgments.
¹³⁸ Thy testimonies that thou hast commanded
      are righteous and very faithful.
¹³⁹ My zeal hath consumed me,
      because mine enemies have forgotten thy words.
¹⁴⁰ Thy word is very pure;
      therefore thy servant loveth it.
¹⁴¹ I am small and despised;
      yet do not I forget thy precepts.
¹⁴² Thy righteousness is an everlasting righteousness,
      and thy law is the truth.

¹⁴³ Trouble and anguish have taken hold on me;
yet thy commandments are my delights.
¹⁴⁴ The righteousness of thy testimonies is everlasting:
give me understanding, and I shall live.

KOPH

¹⁴⁵ I cried with my whole heart;
hear me, O Lord: I will keep thy statutes.
¹⁴⁶ I cried unto thee;
save me, and I shall keep thy testimonies.
¹⁴⁷ I prevented the dawning of the morning,
and cried: 'I hoped in thy word.'
¹⁴⁸ Mine eyes prevent the night watches,
that I might meditate in thy word.
¹⁴⁹ Hear my voice according unto thy lovingkindness:
'O Lord, quicken me according to thy judgment.'
¹⁵⁰ They draw nigh that follow after mischief:
they are far from thy law.
¹⁵¹ Thou art near, O Lord;
and all thy commandments are truth.
¹⁵² Concerning thy testimonies,
I have known of old that thou hast founded
them for ever.

RESH

¹⁵³ Consider mine affliction, and deliver me;
for I do not forget thy law.
¹⁵⁴ Plead my cause, and deliver me:
quicken me according to thy word.

¹⁵⁵ Salvation is far from the wicked;
    for they seek not thy statutes.
¹⁵⁶ Great are thy tender mercies, O Lord:
    quicken me according to thy judgments.
¹⁵⁷ Many are my persecutors and mine enemies;
    yet do I not decline from thy testimonies.
¹⁵⁸ I beheld the transgressors, and was grieved;
    because they kept not thy word.
¹⁵⁹ Consider how I love thy precepts:
    quicken me, O Lord, according to thy
        lovingkindness.
¹⁶⁰ Thy word is true from the beginning;
    and every one of thy righteous judgments
        endureth for ever.

SCHIN

¹⁶¹ Princes have persecuted me without a cause;
    but my heart standeth in awe of thy word.
¹⁶² I rejoice at thy word,
    as one that findeth great spoil.
¹⁶³ I hate and abhor lying;
    but thy law do I love.
¹⁶⁴ Seven times a day do I praise thee
    because of thy righteous judgments.
¹⁶⁵ Great peace have they which love thy law;
    and nothing shall offend them.
¹⁶⁶ Lord, I have hoped for thy salvation,
    and done thy commandments.

¹⁶⁷ My soul hath kept thy testimonies;
　　and I love them exceedingly.
¹⁶⁸ I have kept thy precepts and thy testimonies;
　　for all my ways are before thee.

TAU

¹⁶⁹ Let my cry come near before thee, O Lord:
　　give me understanding according to thy word.
¹⁷⁰ Let my supplication come before thee:
　　deliver me according to thy word.
¹⁷¹ My lips shall utter praise,
　　when thou hast taught me thy statutes.
¹⁷² My tongue shall speak of thy word;
　　for all thy commandments are righteousness.
¹⁷³ Let thine hand help me;
　　for I have chosen thy precepts.
¹⁷⁴ I have longed for thy salvation, O Lord;
　　and thy law is my delight.
¹⁷⁵ Let my soul live, and it shall praise thee;
　　and let thy judgments help me.
¹⁷⁶ I have gone astray like a lost sheep;
　　seek thy servant;
　　　　for I do not forget thy commandments.

120

A song of degrees.

In my distress I cried unto the Lord,
　　and he heard me,

²'Deliver my soul, O Lord,
    from lying lips, and from a deceitful tongue.'
³ What shall be given unto thee?
    Or what shall be done unto thee,
        thou false tongue?
⁴ Sharp arrows of the mighty,
    with coals of juniper.
⁵ Woe is me, that I sojourn in Mesech,
    that I dwell in the tents of Kedar!
⁶ My soul hath long dwelt with him
    that hateth peace.
⁷ I am for peace;
    but when I speak, they are for war.

121

A song of degrees.

I will lift up mine eyes unto the hills,
    from whence cometh my help.
² My help cometh from the Lord,
    which made heaven and earth.
³ He will not suffer thy foot to be moved:
    he that keepeth thee will not slumber.
⁴ Behold, he that keepeth Israel shall neither
    slumber nor sleep.
⁵ The Lord is thy keeper:
    the Lord is thy shade upon thy right hand.
⁶ The sun shall not smite thee by day,
    nor the moon by night.

⁷ The Lord shall preserve thee from all evil:
    he shall preserve thy soul.
⁸ The Lord shall preserve thy going out
    and thy coming in from this time forth,
        and even for evermore.

122

A song of degrees of David.

I was glad when they said unto me,
    'Let us go into the house of the Lord.'
² Our feet shall stand within thy gates,
    O Jerusalem.
³ Jerusalem is builded as a city
    that is compact together.
⁴ Whither the tribes go up, the tribes of the Lord,
    unto the testimony of Israel,
        to give thanks unto the name of the Lord.
⁵ For there are set thrones of judgment,
    the thrones of the house of David.
⁶ Pray for the peace of Jerusalem:
    they shall prosper that love thee.
⁷ Peace be within thy walls,
    and prosperity within thy palaces.
⁸ For my brethren and companions' sakes,
    I will now say, 'Peace be within thee.'
⁹ Because of the house of the Lord our God
    I will seek thy good.

123 A song of degrees.

Unto thee lift I up mine eyes,
  O thou that dwellest
  in the heavens.
² Behold, as the eyes of servants look
  unto the hand of their masters,
    and as the eyes of a maiden
  unto the hand of her mistress;
    so our eyes wait upon the Lord our God,
  until that he have mercy upon us.
³ Have mercy upon us, O Lord,
  have mercy upon us;
    for we are exceedingly filled with contempt.
⁴ Our soul is exceedingly filled with
  the scorning of those that are at ease,
    and with the contempt of the proud.

124 A song of degrees of David.

If it had not been the Lord who was on our side,
  now may Israel say;
² if it had not been the Lord who was on our side,
  when men rose up against us,
³ then they had swallowed us up quick,
  when their wrath was kindled against us;
⁴ then the waters had overwhelmed us,
  the stream had gone over our soul;

⁵ then the proud waters had gone over our soul.
⁶ Blessed be the Lord,
    who hath not given us as a prey to their teeth.
⁷ Our soul is escaped as a bird out of the snare
    of the fowlers:
        the snare is broken, and we are escaped.
⁸ Our help is in the name of the Lord,
    who made heaven and earth.

125

A song of degrees.

They that trust in the Lord shall be as mount Zion,
which cannot be removed,
    but abideth for ever.
² As the mountains are round about Jerusalem,
    so the Lord is round about his people
    from henceforth even for ever.
³ For the rod of the wicked shall not rest
    upon the lot of the righteous;
        lest the righteous put forth their hands
    unto iniquity.
⁴ Do good, O Lord, unto those that be good,
    and to them that are upright in their hearts.
⁵ As for such as turn aside unto their crooked ways,
    the Lord shall lead them forth
        with the workers of iniquity;
    but peace shall be upon Israel.

126 A song of degrees.

When the Lord turned again the captivity of Zion,
we were like them that dream.

² Then was our mouth filled with laughter,
and our tongue with singing;

then said they among the heathen,
'The Lord hath done great things for them.'

³ The Lord hath done great things for us;
whereof we are glad.

⁴ Turn again our captivity, O Lord,
as the streams in the south.

⁵ They that sow in tears shall reap in joy.

⁶ He that goeth forth and weepeth,
bearing precious seed,

shall doubtless come again with rejoicing,
bringing his sheaves with him.

127 A song of degrees for Solomon.

Except the Lord build the house,
they labour in vain that build it;

except the Lord keep the city,
the watchman waketh but in vain.

² It is vain for you to rise up early,
to sit up late, to eat the bread of sorrows;

for so he giveth his beloved sleep.

³ Lo, children are an heritage of the Lord;
   and the fruit of the womb
      is his reward.
⁴ As arrows are in the hand of a mighty man;
   so are children of the youth.
⁵ Happy is the man that hath his quiver full of them:
   they shall not be ashamed,
      but they shall speak with the enemies
   in the gate.

128

A song of degrees.

Blessed is every one that feareth the Lord;
   that walketh in his ways.
² For thou shalt eat the labour of thine hands:
   happy shalt thou be,
      and it shall be well with thee.
³ Thy wife shall be as a fruitful vine by the sides
   of thine house: thy children like olive plants
      round about thy table.
⁴ Behold, that thus shall the man be blessed
   that feareth the Lord.
⁵ The Lord shall bless thee out of Zion;
   and thou shalt see the good of Jerusalem
      all the days of thy life.
⁶ Yea, thou shalt see thy children's children,
   and peace upon Israel.

129

A song of degrees.

'Many a time have they afflicted me
   from my youth,'
may Israel now say:
[2] 'Many a time have they afflicted me
   from my youth;
      yet they have not prevailed against me.
[3] The plowers plowed upon my back:
   they made long their furrows.'
[4] The Lord is righteous:
   he hath cut asunder the cords of the wicked.
[5] Let them all be confounded and turned back
   that hate Zion.
[6] Let them be as the grass upon the housetops,
   which withereth afore it groweth up;
[7] wherewith the mower filleth not his hand;
   nor he that bindeth sheaves his bosom.
[8] Neither do they which go by say,
   'The blessing of the Lord be upon you:
      we bless you in the name of the Lord.'

130

A song of degrees.

Out of the depths have I cried unto thee, O Lord.
[2] Lord, hear my voice: let thine ears be attentive
   to the voice of my supplications.

³ If thou, Lord, shouldest mark inquities,
  O Lord, who shall stand?
⁴ But there is forgiveness with thee,
  that thou mayest be feared.
⁵ I wait for the Lord, my soul doth wait,
  and in his word do I hope.
⁶ My soul waiteth for the Lord more than they that
  watch for the morning:
    I say, more than they that watch
  for the morning.
⁷ Let Israel hope in the Lord;
  for with the Lord there is mercy,
    and with him is plenteous redemption.
⁸ And he shall redeem Israel
  from all his iniquities.

131 A song of degrees of David.

Lord, my heart is not haughty, nor mine eyes lofty;
    neither do I exercise myself in great matters,
  or in things too high for me.
² Surely I have behaved and quieted myself,
  as a child that is weaned of his mother:
    my soul is even as a weaned child.
³ Let Israel hope in the Lord from henceforth
  and for ever.

132

A song of degrees.

Lord, remember David, and all his afflictions:
[2] how he sware unto the Lord,
  and vowed unto the mighty God of Jacob;
[3] surely I will not come into the tabernacle
  of my house, nor go up into my bed;
[4] I will not give sleep to mine eyes,
  or slumber to mine eyelids,
[5] until I find out a place for the Lord,
  an habitation for the mighty God of Jacob.
[6] Lo, we heard of it at Ephratah:
  we found it in the fields of the wood.
[7] 'We will go into his tabernacles:
  we will worship at his footstool.'
[8] Arise, O Lord, into thy rest;
  thou, and the ark of thy strength.
[9] Let thy priests be clothed with righteousness;
  and let thy saints shout for joy.
[10] For thy servant David's sake
  turn not away the face of thine anointed.
[11] The Lord hath sworn in truth unto David;
  he will not turn from it:
    'Of the fruit of thy body will I set upon
  thy throne.
[12] If thy children will keep my covenant
  and my testimony that I shall teach them,
    their children shall also sit upon
  thy throne for evermore.'

¹³ For the Lord hath chosen Zion;
>> he hath desired it for his habitation.
¹⁴ This is my rest for ever:
>> here will I dwell;
>>> for I have desired it.
¹⁵ I will abundantly bless her provision:
>> I will satisfy her poor with bread.
¹⁶ I will also clothe her priests with salvation;
>> and her saints shall shout aloud for joy.
¹⁷ There will I make the horn of David to bud:
>> I have ordained a lamp for mine anointed.
¹⁸ His enemies will I clothe with shame;
>> but upon himself
>>> shall his crown flourish.

133

A song of degrees of David.

Behold, how good and how pleasant it is
>> for brethren to dwell together in unity!
² It is like the precious ointment upon the head,
>> that ran down upon the beard,
>>> even Aaron's beard;
>> that went down to the skirts of his garments;
³ as the dew of Hermon,
>> and as the dew that descended upon
>>> the mountains of Zion;
>> for there the Lord commanded the blessing,
>>> even life for evermore.

134

A song of degrees.

Behold, bless ye the Lord,
    all ye servants of the Lord,
  which by night stand in the house of the Lord.
2 Lift up your hands in the sanctuary,
    and bless the Lord.
3 The Lord that made heaven and earth
    bless thee out of Zion.

135

Praise ye the Lord.
    Praise ye the name of the Lord; praise him,
    O ye servants of the Lord.
2 Ye that stand in the house of the Lord,
    in the courts of the house of our God,
3 praise the Lord, for the Lord is good;
    sing praises unto his name, for it is pleasant.
4 For the Lord hath chosen Jacob unto himself,
    and Israel for his peculiar treasure.
5 For I know that the Lord is great,
    and that our Lord is above all gods.
6 Whatsoever the Lord pleased,
    that did he in heaven, and in earth,
      in the seas, and all deep places.
7 He causeth the vapours to ascend from
    the ends of the earth;
      he maketh lightnings for the rain;
      he bringeth the wind out of his treasuries.

⁸ Who smote the firstborn of Egypt,
    both of man and beast.
⁹ Who sent tokens and wonders into the midst
    of thee, O Egypt, upon Pharaoh,
        and upon all his servants.
¹⁰ Who smote great nations, and slew mighty kings;
¹¹ Sihon king of the Amorites, and Og king of Bashan,
    and all the kingdoms of Canaan;
¹² and gave their land for an heritage,
    an heritage unto Israel his people.
¹³ Thy name, O Lord, endureth for ever;
    and thy memorial, O Lord,
        throughout all generations.
¹⁴ For the Lord will judge his people,
    and he will repent himself concerning
        his servants.
¹⁵ The idols of the heathen are silver and gold,
    the work of men's hands.
¹⁶ They have mouths, but they speak not;
    eyes have they, but they see not;
¹⁷ they have ears, but they hear not;
    neither is there any breath in their mouths.
¹⁸ They that make them are like unto them:
    so is every one that trusteth in them.
¹⁹ Bless the Lord, O house of Israel;
    bless the Lord, O house of Aaron;
²⁰ bless the Lord, O house of Levi;
    ye that fear the Lord, bless the Lord.

²¹ Blessed be the Lord out of Zion,
which dwelleth at Jerusalem.
Praise ye the Lord.

136 O Give thanks unto the Lord; for he is good;
for his mercy endureth for ever.
² O give thanks unto the God of gods;
for his mercy endureth for ever.
³ O give thanks to the Lord of lords;
for his mercy endureth for ever.
⁴ To him who alone doeth great wonders;
for his mercy endureth for ever.
⁵ To him that by wisdom made the heavens;
for his mercy endureth for ever.
⁶ To him that stretched out the earth
above the waters;
for his mercy endureth for ever.
⁷ To him that made great lights;
for his mercy endureth for ever:
⁸ the sun to rule by day;
for his mercy endureth for ever:
⁹ the moon and stars to rule by night;
for his mercy endureth for ever.
¹⁰ To him that smote Egypt in their firstborn;
for his mercy endureth for ever;
¹¹ and brought out Israel from among them;
for his mercy endureth for ever;

¹² with a strong hand, and with a stretched out arm;
   for his mercy endureth for ever.
¹³ To him which divided the Red sea into parts;
   for his mercy endureth for ever;
¹⁴ and made Israel to pass through the midst of it;
   for his mercy endureth for ever;
¹⁵ but overthrew Pharaoh and his host in the Red sea;
   for his mercy endureth for ever.
¹⁶ To him which led his people
   through the wilderness;
      for his mercy endureth for ever.
¹⁷ To him which smote great kings;
   for his mercy endureth for ever;
¹⁸ and slew famous kings;
   for his mercy endureth for ever;
¹⁹ Sihon king of the Amorites;
   for his mercy endureth for ever;
²⁰ and Og the king of Bashan;
   for his mercy endureth for ever;
²¹ and gave their land for an heritage;
   for his mercy endureth for ever;
²² even an heritage unto Israel his servant;
   for his mercy endureth for ever.
²³ Who remembered us in our low estate;
   for his mercy endureth for ever;
²⁴ and hath redeemed us from our enemies;
   for his mercy endureth for ever.
²⁵ Who giveth food to all flesh;

for his mercy endureth for ever.
²⁶ O give thanks unto the God of heaven;
    for his mercy endureth for ever.

137 By the rivers of Babylon, there we sat down,
    yea, we wept, when we remembered Zion.
² We hanged our harps upon the willows
    in the midst thereof.
³ For there they that carried us away captive
    required of us a song;
        and they that wasted us required of us mirth,
    saying, 'Sing us one of the songs of Zion.'
⁴ How shall we sing the Lord's song
    in a strange land?
⁵ If I forget thee, O Jerusalem,
    let my right hand forget her cunning.
⁶ If I do not remember thee,
    let my tongue cleave to the roof of my mouth;
        if I prefer not Jerusalem above my chief joy.
⁷ Remember, O Lord,
    the children of Edom in the day of Jerusalem;
        who said, 'Rase it, rase it,
    even to the foundation thereof.'
⁸ O daughter of Babylon, who art to be destroyed;
    happy shall he be, that rewardeth thee
        as thou hast served us.

⁹ Happy shall he be,
>   that taketh and dasheth thy little ones
>   against the stones.

138 A psalm of David.

I will praise thee with my whole heart:
>   before the gods will I sing praise unto thee.
² I will worship toward thy holy temple,
>   and praise thy name for thy loving-kindness
>   and for thy truth;
>   for thou hast magnified thy word above
>   all thy name.
³ In the day when I cried thou answeredst me,
>   and strengthenedst me with strength
>   in my soul.
⁴ All the kings of the earth shall praise thee, O Lord,
>   when they hear the words of thy mouth.
⁵ Yea, they shall sing in the ways of the Lord;
>   for great is the glory of the Lord.
⁶ Though the Lord be high,
>   yet hath he respect unto the lowly;
>   but the proud he knoweth afar off.
⁷ Though I walk in the midst of trouble,
>   thou wilt revive me;
>   thou shalt stretch forth thine hand
>   against the wrath of mine enemies,
>   and thy right hand shall save me.

⁸ The Lord will perfect that which concerneth me:
thy mercy, O Lord, endureth for ever:
forsake not the works of thine own hands.

139

To the chief musician, a psalm of David.

O Lord, thou hast searched me,
and known me.
² Thou knowest my downsitting and mine uprising,
thou understandest my thought afar off.
³ Thou compassest my path and my lying down,
and art acquainted with all my ways.
⁴ For there is not a word in my tongue,
but, lo, O Lord, thou knowest it altogether.
⁵ Thou hast beset me behind and before,
and laid thine hand upon me.
⁶ Such knowledge is too wonderful for me;
it is high, I cannot attain unto it.
⁷ Whither shall I go from thy spirit?
Or whither shall I flee from thy presence?
⁸ If I ascend up into heaven, thou art there:
if I make my bed in hell, behold, thou art there.
⁹ If I take the wings of the morning,
and dwell in the uttermost parts of the sea;
¹⁰ even there shall thy hand lead me,
and thy right hand shall hold me.
¹¹ If I say, 'Surely the darkness shall cover me;
even the night shall be light about me.'

¹² Yea, the darkness hideth not from thee;
> but the night shineth as the day;
>> the darkness and the light are both
>> alike to thee.

¹³ For thou hast possessed my reins:
> thou hast covered me in my mother's womb.

¹⁴ I will praise thee;
> for I am fearfully and wonderfully made;
>> marvellous are thy works;
> and that my soul knoweth right well.

¹⁵ My substance was not hid from thee,
> when I was made in secret,
>> and curiously wrought in the lowest parts
> of the earth.

¹⁶ Thine eyes did see my substance,
> yet being unperfect; and in thy book
>> all my members were written,
> which in continuance were fashioned when as
>> yet there was none of them.

¹⁷ How precious also are thy thoughts unto me,
> O God! How great is the sum of them!

¹⁸ If I should count them, they are more in number
> than the sand:
>> when I awake, I am still with thee.

¹⁹ Surely thou wilt slay the wicked, O God:
> depart from me therefore, ye bloody men.

²⁰ For they speak against thee wickedly,
> and thine enemies take thy name in vain.

²¹ Do not I hate them, O Lord, that hate thee?
    And am not I grieved with those that rise up
        against thee?
²² I hate them with perfect hatred:
    I count them mine enemies.
²³ Search me, O God, and know my heart:
    try me, and know my thoughts:
²⁴ and see if there be any wicked way in me,
    and lead me in the way everlasting.

140

To the chief musician, a psalm of David.

Deliver me, O Lord, from the evil man:
    preserve me from the violent man;
² which imagine mischiefs in their heart;
    continually are they gathered together for war.
³ They have sharpened their tongues like a serpent;
    adders' poison is under their lips. Selah.
⁴ Keep me, O Lord, from the hands of the wicked;
    preserve me from the violent man;
        who have purposed to overthrow my goings.
⁵ The proud have hid a snare for me, and cords;
    they have spread a net by the wayside;
        they have set gins for me. Selah.
⁶ I said unto the Lord, 'Thou art my God:
    hear the voice of my supplications, O Lord.'
⁷ O God the Lord, the strength of my salvation,
    thou hast covered my head
        in the day of battle.

⁸ Grant not, O Lord, the desires of the wicked:
    further not his wicked device;
        lest they exalt themselves. Selah.
⁹ As for the head of those that compass me about,
    let the mischief of their own lips cover them.
¹⁰ Let burning coals fall upon them;
    let them be cast into the fire;
        into deep pits, that they rise not up again.
¹¹ Let not an evil speaker be established in the earth:
    evil shall hunt the violent man to overthrow him.
¹² I know that the Lord will maintain
    the cause of the afflicted, and the right
        of the poor.
¹³ Surely the righteous shall give thanks
    unto thy name:
        the upright shall dwell in thy presence.

141 A psalm of David.

    Lord, I cry unto thee: make haste unto me;
        give ear unto my voice,
    when I cry unto thee.
² Let my prayer be set forth before thee as incense;
    and the lifting up of my hands
        as the evening sacrifice.
³ Set a watch, O Lord, before my mouth;
    keep the door of my lips.
⁴ Incline not my heart to any evil thing,

to practise wicked works with men
      that work iniquity;
and let me not eat of their dainties.
⁵ Let the righteous smite me;
      it shall be a kindness; and let him reprove me;
            it shall be an excellent oil,
      which shall not break my head;
            for yet my prayer also
      shall be in their calamities.
⁶ When their judges are overthrown in stony places,
      they shall hear my words; for they are sweet.
⁷ Our bones are scattered at the grave's mouth,
      as when one cutteth and cleaveth wood
            upon the earth.
⁸ But mine eyes are unto thee, O God the Lord:
      in thee is my trust; leave not my soul destitute.
⁹ Keep me from the snares
      which they have laid for me,
            and the gins of the workers of iniquity.
¹⁰ Let the wicked fall into their own nets,
      whilst that I withal escape.

142 Maschil of David; a prayer when he was
            in the cave.

I cried unto the Lord with my voice;
      with my voice unto the Lord
            did I make my supplication.

²I poured out my complaint before him;
  I shewed before him my trouble.
³When my spirit was overwhelmed within me,
    then thou knewest my path.
      In the way wherein I walked
      have they privily laid a snare for me.
⁴I looked on my right hand, and beheld,
    but there was no man that would know me;
      refuge failed me;
      no man cared for my soul.
⁵I cried unto thee, O Lord; I said,
    'Thou art my refuge and my portion
      in the land of the living.'
⁶Attend unto my cry; for I am brought very low;
    deliver me from my persecutors;
      for they are stronger than I.
⁷Bring my soul out of prison, that I may praise
    thy name;
      the righteous shall compass me about;
      for thou shalt deal bountifully with me.

143

A psalm of David.

Hear my prayer, O Lord,
    give ear to my supplications:
in thy faithfulness answer me,
    and in thy righteousness.

² And enter not into judgment with thy servant;
    for in thy sight shall no man living
        be justified.
³ For the enemy hath persecuted my soul;
    he hath smitten my life down to the ground;
        he hath made me to dwell in darkness,
    as those that have been long dead.
⁴ Therefore is my spirit overwhelmed within me;
    my heart within me is desolate.
⁵ I remember the days of old;
    I meditate on all thy works;
        I muse on the work of thy hands.
⁶ I stretch forth my hands unto thee:
    my soul thirsteth after thee,
        as a thirsty land. Selah.
⁷ Hear me speedily, O Lord: my spirit faileth:
    hide not thy face from me, lest I be like unto
        them that go down into the pit.
⁸ Cause me to hear thy lovingkindness in
    the morning; for in thee do I trust:
        cause me to know the way wherein
    I should walk; for I lift up my soul
        unto thee.
⁹ Deliver me, O Lord, from mine enemies:
    I flee unto thee to hide me.
¹⁰ Teach me to do thy will;
    for thou art my God: thy spirit is good;
        lead me into the land of uprightness.

[11] Quicken me, O Lord, for thy name's sake;
  for thy righteousness' sake bring my soul
    out of trouble.
[12] And of thy mercy cut off mine enemies,
  and destroy all them that afflict my soul;
    for I am thy servant.

144

A psalm of David.

Blessed be the Lord my strength,
  which teacheth my hands to war,
and my fingers to fight:
[2] my goodness, and my fortress;
  my high tower, and my deliverer;
    my shield, and he in whom I trust;
  who subdueth my people under me.
[3] Lord, what is man,
  that thou takest knowledge of him!
    Or the son of man, that thou makest
  account of him!
[4] Man is like to vanity:
  his days are as a shadow
    that passeth away.
[5] Bow thy heavens, O Lord, and come down:
  touch the mountains, and they shall smoke.
[6] Cast forth lightning, and scatter them:
  shoot out thine arrows, and destroy them.

⁷ Send thine hand from above;
>rid me, and deliver me out of great waters,
>>from the hand of strange children;
⁸ whose mouth speaketh vanity,
>and their right hand is a right hand of falsehood.
⁹ I will sing a new song unto thee, O God:
>upon a psaltery and an instrument of ten strings
>>will I sing praises unto thee.
¹⁰ It is he that giveth salvation unto kings,
>who delivereth David his servant from
>>the hurtful sword.
¹¹ Rid me, and deliver me from the hand
>of strange children, whose mouth speaketh vanity,
>>and their right hand is a right hand of
>>falsehood.
¹² That our sons may be as plants grown up
>in their youth;
>>that our daughters may be as corner stones,
>polished after the similitude of a palace;
¹³ that our garners may be full,
>affording all manner of store;
>>that our sheep may bring forth thousands
>and ten thousands in our streets;
¹⁴ that our oxen may be strong to labour;
>that there be no breaking in, nor going out;
>>that there be no complaining in our streets.
¹⁵ Happy is that people, that is in such a case;
>yea, happy is that people, whose God is the Lord.

145

David's psalm of praise.

I will extol thee, my God, O king;
>and I will bless thy name for ever and ever.
[2] Every day will I bless thee;
>and I will praise thy name for ever and ever.
[3] Great is the Lord, and greatly to be praised;
>and his greatness is unsearchable.
[4] One generation shall praise thy works to another,
>and shall declare thy mighty acts.
[5] I will speak of the glorious honour of thy majesty,
>and of thy wondrous works.
[6] And men shall speak of the might
>of thy terrible acts;
>>and I will declare thy greatness.
[7] They shall abundantly utter the memory
>of thy great goodness,
>>and shall sing of thy righteousness.
[8] The Lord is gracious, and full of compassion;
>slow to anger, and of great mercy.
[9] The Lord is good to all;
>and his tender mercies are over all his works.
[10] All thy works shall praise thee, O Lord;
>and thy saints shall bless thee.
[11] They shall speak of the glory of thy kingdom,
>and talk of thy power;
[12] to make known to the sons of men his mighty acts,
>and the glorious majesty of his kingdom.

¹³ Thy kingdom is an everlasting kingdom,
   and thy dominion endureth throughout
      all generations.
¹⁴ The Lord upholdeth all that fall,
   and raiseth up all those that be bowed down.
¹⁵ The eyes of all wait upon thee;
   and thou givest them their meat in due season.
¹⁶ Thou openest thine hand,
   and satisfiest the desire of every living thing.
¹⁷ The Lord is righteous in all his ways,
   and holy in all his works.
¹⁸ The Lord is nigh unto all them that call upon him,
   to all that call upon him in truth.
¹⁹ He will fulfil the desire of them that fear him;
   he also will hear their cry, and will save them.
²⁰ The Lord preserveth all them that love him;
   but all the wicked will he destroy.
²¹ My mouth shall speak the praise of the Lord;
   and let all flesh bless his holy name
      for ever and ever.

146 Praise ye the Lord. Praise the Lord, O my soul.
   ² While I live will I praise the Lord:
      I will sing praises unto my God while I have
   any being.
³ Put not your trust in princes, nor in
   the son of man, in whom there is no help.

⁴His breath goeth forth, he returneth to his earth;
    in that very day his thoughts perish.
⁵Happy is he that hath the God of Jacob for his help,
    whose hope is in the Lord his God,
⁶which made heaven, and earth, the sea,
        and all that therein is;
            which keepeth truth for ever;
⁷which executeth judgment for the oppressed;
        which giveth food to the hungry.
        The Lord looseth the prisoners.
⁸The Lord openeth the eyes of the blind;
        the Lord raiseth them that are bowed down;
            the Lord loveth the righteous;
⁹the Lord preserveth the strangers;
        he relieveth the fatherless and widow;
            but the way of the wicked
            he turneth upside down.
¹⁰The Lord shall reign for ever,
        even thy God, O Zion, unto all generations.
            Praise ye the Lord.

147 Praise ye the Lord;
        for it is good to sing praises unto our God;
    for it is pleasant; and praise is comely.
²The Lord doth build up Jerusalem:
    he gathereth together the outcasts of Israel.
³He healeth the broken in heart,
    and bindeth up their wounds.

⁴ He telleth the number of the stars;
  he calleth them all by their names.
⁵ Great is our Lord, and of great power:
  his understanding is infinite.
⁶ The Lord lifteth up the meek:
  he casteth the wicked down to the ground.
⁷ Sing unto the Lord with thanksgiving;
  sing praise upon the harp unto our God,
⁸ who covereth the heaven with clouds,
  who prepareth rain for the earth,
    who maketh grass to grow upon
    the mountains.
⁹ He giveth to the beast his food,
  and to the young ravens which cry.
¹⁰ He delighteth not in the strength of the horse:
  he taketh not pleasure in the legs of a man.
¹¹ The Lord taketh pleasure in them that fear him,
  in those that hope in his mercy.
¹² Praise the Lord, O Jerusalem;
  praise thy God, O Zion.
¹³ For he hath strengthened the bars of thy gates;
  he hath blessed thy children within thee.
¹⁴ He maketh peace in thy borders,
  and filleth thee with the finest of the wheat.
¹⁵ He sendeth forth his commandment upon earth:
  his word runneth very swiftly.
¹⁶ He giveth snow like wool:
  he scattereth the hoarfrost like ashes.

¹⁷ He casteth forth his ice like morsels.
  Who can stand before his cold?
¹⁸ He sendeth out his word, and melteth them:
  he causeth his wind to blow, and the waters flow.
¹⁹ He sheweth his word unto Jacob,
  his statutes and his judgments
    unto Israel.
²⁰ He hath not dealt so with any nation;
  and as for his judgments,
    they have not known them.
  Praise ye the Lord.

148

Praise ye the Lord.
  Praise ye the Lord from the heavens:
  praise him in the heights.
² Praise ye him, all his angels:
  praise ye him, all his hosts.
³ Praise ye him, sun and moon:
  praise him, all ye stars of light.
⁴ Praise him, ye heavens of heavens,
  and ye waters that be above the heavens.
⁵ Let them praise the name of the Lord;
  for he commanded, and they were created.
⁶ He hath also stablished them for ever and ever:
  he hath made a decree which shall not pass.
⁷ Praise the Lord from the earth,
  ye dragons, and all deeps;

⁸ fire, and hail; snow, and vapour;
  stormy wind fulfilling his word.
⁹ Mountains, and all hills;
  fruitful trees, and all cedars;
¹⁰ beasts, and all cattle;
  creeping things, and flying fowl.
¹¹ Kings of the earth, and all people;
  princes, and all judges of the earth;
¹² both young men, and maidens;
  old men, and children.
¹³ Let them praise the name of the Lord;
  for his name alone is excellent;
    his glory is above the earth and heaven.
¹⁴ He also exalteth the horn of his people,
  the praise of all his saints;
    even of the children of Israel,
  a people near unto him. Praise ye the Lord.

149 Praise ye the Lord.
    Sing unto the Lord a new song,
  and his praise in the congregation of saints.
² Let Israel rejoice in him that made him:
  let the children of Zion be joyful in their King.
³ Let them praise his name in the dance:
  let them sing praises unto him
    with the timbrel and harp.
⁴ For the Lord taketh pleasure in his people:
  he will beautify the meek with salvation.

⁵ Let the saints be joyful in glory:
   let them sing aloud upon their beds.
⁶ Let the high praises of God be in their mouth,
   and a twoedged sword in their hand;
⁷ to execute vengeance upon the heathen,
   and punishments upon the people;
⁸ to bind their kings with chains,
   and their nobles with fetters of iron;
⁹ to execute upon them the judgment written:
   this honour have all his saints.
      Praise ye the Lord.

150

Praise ye the Lord.
   Praise God in his sanctuary:
praise him in the firmament of his power.
² Praise him for his mighty acts:
   praise him according to his excellent greatness.
³ Praise him with the sound of the trumpet:
   praise him with the psaltery and harp.
⁴ Praise him with the timbrel and dance:
   praise him with stringed instruments and organs.
⁵ Praise him upon the loud cymbals:
   praise him upon the high sounding cymbals.
⁶ Let every thing that hath breath praise the Lord.
   Praise ye the Lord.

the pocket canons

All of the above titles can be ordered directly from:
Canongate Books, 14 High Street, Edinburgh EH1 1TE
Tel 0131 557 5111 Fax 0131 557 5211